60 Caribbean & West Indian Recipes for Home

By: Kelly Johnson

Table of Contents

Appetizers and Snacks:

- Jamaican Beef Patties: Spiced beef filling encased in a flaky pastry.
- Accra (Saltfish Fritters): Fried dough with salted cod.
- Trinidadian Doubles: Curried chickpeas sandwiched between two fried bread pieces.
- Conch Fritters: Fried dough with tender conch pieces.

Main Courses:

- Jamaican Jerk Chicken: Chicken marinated in a spicy jerk seasoning.
- Curry Goat: Tender goat meat slow-cooked in a flavorful curry sauce.
- Roti: Flatbread with various fillings like curried chicken, shrimp, or vegetables.
- Bahamian Rock Lobster Tail: Grilled or baked lobster tail with island spices.
- Ackee and Saltfish: Jamaica's national dish featuring ackee fruit and salted cod.
- Pelau: One-pot rice dish with meat, rice, and pigeon peas.
- Bajan Flying Fish Cou-Cou: Cornmeal and okra dish with flying fish.
- Guyanese Pepper Pot: Cassava soup with meat and spices.
- Stewed Conch: Conch cooked in a savory tomato-based sauce.

Vegetarian and Vegan Delights:

- Vegan Callaloo: Leafy greens stewed with coconut milk.
- Vegetarian Roti: Flatbread with flavorful vegetable fillings.
- Rasta Pasta: Pasta dish with a creamy coconut milk sauce and veggies.

- Trinidadian Aloo Pie: Fried or baked potato pies with spiced fillings.
- Jamaican Ital Stew: Vegan stew with vegetables and coconut milk.

Seafood Specialities:

- Grilled Caribbean Spiny Lobster: Lobster grilled with Caribbean spices.
- Jamaican Brown Stew Fish: Fish marinated and stewed in a rich, brown sauce.
- Belizean Ceviche: Fresh seafood cured in citrus juices.
- Curried Crab and Dumplings: Crab cooked in a curry sauce with dumplings.
- Dominican Mangu with Shrimp: Mashed plantains with seasoned shrimp.

Side Dishes and Condiments:

- Coconut Rice and Peas: Rice cooked with coconut milk and kidney beans.
- Festival: Sweet fried dough served as a side or snack.
- Callaloo Soup: Leafy green soup with okra and various vegetables.
- Breadfruit Salad: Roasted or boiled breadfruit tossed with herbs and spices.
- Green Fig (Banana) Salad: Green bananas cooked and tossed in a spicy salad.

Desserts and Sweets:

- Rum Cake: Moist cake soaked in rum syrup.
- Guava Duff: Guava-filled dumplings steamed or boiled.
- Tamarind Balls: Tamarind paste rolled into sweet and tangy balls.
- Sorrel Drink: Refreshing drink made from dried sorrel petals.
- Gizzarda: Sweet coconut-filled pastries.

Beverages:

- Punch de Creme: A Trinidadian version of eggnog with rum.
- Mauby: A traditional Caribbean beverage made from the bark of the mauby tree.
- Soursop Juice: Refreshing tropical fruit juice.
- Pineapple Ginger Punch: Pineapple and ginger blended into a sweet and spicy drink.

Preserves and Pickles:

- Mango Chutney: Spiced mango condiment.
- Pepper Sauce: Fiery hot sauce made with local peppers.
- Sorrel Jam: Sweet jam made from sorrel petals.
- Pickled Green Papaya: Tangy pickled green papaya.

Street Food Classics:

- Jamaican Beef Soup: Hearty soup with beef and vegetables.
- Trinidadian Corn Soup: Corn soup with dumplings and provision.
- Bahamian Conch Salad: Fresh conch salad with citrus and spices.
- Bake and Shark: Fried shark sandwich with various toppings.

Breakfast and Brunch:

- Doubles: Fried bread with curried chickpeas.
- Jamaican Bammy: Cassava flatbread served with fish or ackee.
- Belizean Johnny Cakes: Fried dough served with various accompaniments.

Grilled Delicacies:

- Jamaican Escovitch Fish: Fried fish topped with spicy pickled vegetables.
- Bajan Fish Cutter: Fried fish sandwich with Bajan hot sauce.
- Antiguan Pepperpot: Spiced pork stew.

Celebration Dishes:

- Bajan Black Cake: Dark fruitcake soaked in rum.
- Guyanese Pepperpot: Spicy meat stew traditionally served at Christmas.
- Jamaican Sorrel Chicken: Chicken cooked in a sorrel-infused sauce.

Local Flavors:

- Green Seasoning: Blend of fresh herbs and spices used as a marinade.
- Belizean Rice and Beans: Classic rice and beans dish cooked in coconut milk.
- Curry Crab and Dumplings: Crab cooked in a flavorful curry sauce.
- St. Lucian Bread Pudding: Sweet bread pudding with local spices.

Unique Treats:

- Jamaican Solomon Gundy: Spicy fish spread.
- Puerto Rican Mofongo: Mashed plantains with garlic and pork.

Appetizers and Snacks:

Jamaican Beef Patties: Spiced beef filling encased in a flaky pastry.

Ingredients:

For the Pastry:

- 3 cups all-purpose flour
- 1 cup cold unsalted butter, cut into small cubes
- 1 teaspoon turmeric powder (for color)
- 1 teaspoon salt
- 1/2 cup ice water

For the Filling:

- 1 pound ground beef
- 1 medium onion, finely chopped
- 2 cloves garlic, minced
- 1 teaspoon fresh thyme, chopped
- 1 teaspoon curry powder
- 1/2 teaspoon ground allspice
- 1/2 teaspoon paprika
- 1/2 teaspoon turmeric powder (for color)
- Salt and pepper to taste
- 1/4 cup breadcrumbs
- 1/4 cup beef or vegetable broth

Instructions:

Prepare the Pastry:
- In a large bowl, combine the flour, turmeric powder, and salt. Add the cold, cubed butter.
- Use your fingertips to rub the butter into the flour until the mixture resembles coarse crumbs.
- Gradually add the ice water and knead the dough until it comes together. Form the dough into a ball, wrap it in plastic wrap, and refrigerate for at least 30 minutes.

Prepare the Filling:

- In a skillet over medium heat, cook the ground beef until browned. Drain excess fat if necessary.
- Add chopped onions, minced garlic, fresh thyme, curry powder, ground allspice, paprika, turmeric powder, salt, and pepper. Cook until the onions are softened.
- Stir in the breadcrumbs and beef or vegetable broth. Simmer until the mixture thickens. Remove from heat and let it cool.

Assemble the Patties:
- Preheat the oven to 375°F (190°C).
- Roll out the chilled pastry on a floured surface to about 1/8-inch thickness. Cut circles about 5-6 inches in diameter.
- Spoon a generous portion of the beef filling onto one half of each pastry circle, leaving a border.
- Fold the other half of the pastry over the filling, forming a half-moon shape. Press the edges to seal, and use a fork to crimp the edges.

Bake the Patties:
- Place the assembled patties on a baking sheet lined with parchment paper.
- Bake in the preheated oven for 25-30 minutes or until the pastry is golden brown.

Serve:
- Allow the patties to cool slightly before serving. They can be enjoyed warm or at room temperature.

Enjoy these Jamaican Beef Patties as a flavorful snack or meal!

Accra (Saltfish Fritters): Fried dough with salted cod.

Ingredients:

- 1 cup salted codfish, soaked and flaked
- 1 cup all-purpose flour
- 1 teaspoon baking powder
- 1/2 teaspoon ground black pepper
- 1/2 teaspoon cayenne pepper (adjust to taste)
- 1/2 teaspoon paprika
- 1/2 teaspoon thyme, dried
- 1/2 teaspoon baking soda
- 1 cup chopped scallions (green onions)
- 1/4 cup chopped fresh parsley
- 1 small onion, finely chopped
- 1 teaspoon minced garlic
- 1 cup cold water
- Vegetable oil for frying

Instructions:

Prepare the Saltfish:
- Soak the salted codfish in cold water for at least 4 hours or overnight, changing the water a few times. Boil the soaked codfish for about 10 minutes to remove excess salt. Drain and flake the codfish into small pieces.

Make the Batter:
- In a large mixing bowl, combine the flour, baking powder, black pepper, cayenne pepper, paprika, dried thyme, and baking soda.
- Add the flaked codfish, chopped scallions, parsley, chopped onion, and minced garlic to the dry ingredients. Mix well.
- Gradually add the cold water to the dry ingredients, stirring continuously until you have a thick, smooth batter.

Fry the Accra:
- In a deep pan or fryer, heat enough vegetable oil for deep frying to 350°F (180°C).

- Drop spoonfuls of the batter into the hot oil, forming small fritters. Fry until the fritters are golden brown and crispy, turning them to ensure even cooking. This should take about 3-4 minutes per side.
- Use a slotted spoon to remove the Accra from the oil and place them on a plate lined with paper towels to absorb any excess oil.

Serve:
- Serve the Accra warm as a delightful snack or appetizer.

These Accra (Saltfish Fritters) are a delicious combination of crispy on the outside and flavorful on the inside. Enjoy them with a dipping sauce of your choice, such as hot pepper sauce or a tangy tamarind sauce.

Trinidadian Doubles: Curried chickpeas sandwiched between two fried bread pieces.

Ingredients:

For the Bara (Fried Bread):

- 2 cups all-purpose flour
- 1 teaspoon baking powder
- 1/2 teaspoon ground cumin
- 1/2 teaspoon ground turmeric
- 1/2 teaspoon ground geera (cumin)
- 1 teaspoon yeast
- 1/2 teaspoon sugar
- 1/2 teaspoon salt
- Water (as needed)
- Vegetable oil (for frying)

For the Curried Chickpeas:

- 2 cans (15 ounces each) chickpeas, drained and rinsed
- 1 large onion, finely chopped
- 2 cloves garlic, minced
- 1 tablespoon curry powder
- 1 teaspoon ground cumin
- 1 teaspoon ground turmeric
- 1 teaspoon ground geera (cumin)
- 1 teaspoon hot pepper sauce (adjust to taste)
- 1 cup water
- Salt and pepper to taste
- Chopped cilantro for garnish

Instructions:

For the Bara (Fried Bread):

    Prepare the Dough:
- In a large bowl, combine the flour, baking powder, ground cumin, ground turmeric, ground geera, yeast, sugar, and salt.

- Gradually add water and knead the mixture to form a smooth, elastic dough. Cover the bowl with a damp cloth and let the dough rest for about 1 hour.

Shape and Fry the Bara:
- Pinch off small portions of the dough and shape them into small, round patties.
- Heat vegetable oil in a frying pan over medium-high heat. Fry the bara until they are golden brown on both sides. Remove and drain on paper towels.

For the Curried Chickpeas:

Prepare the Chickpea Filling:
- In a pan, heat some oil over medium heat. Add chopped onions and garlic, sautéing until softened.
- Add curry powder, ground cumin, ground turmeric, and ground geera. Stir to coat the onions and garlic with the spices.
- Add drained chickpeas and hot pepper sauce. Mix well to coat the chickpeas with the spice mixture.
- Pour in water and let the chickpeas simmer for about 15-20 minutes until the mixture thickens. Season with salt and pepper to taste.

Assemble the Doubles:
- Take two bara and sandwich a generous amount of curried chickpeas between them.
- Garnish with chopped cilantro.

Serve:
- Trinidadian Doubles are typically served with tamarind sauce or hot pepper sauce on the side.

Enjoy the Trinidadian Doubles as a flavorful and satisfying street food experience!

Conch Fritters: Fried dough with tender conch pieces.

Ingredients:

- 1 cup conch meat, finely chopped
- 1 cup all-purpose flour
- 1 teaspoon baking powder
- 1/2 teaspoon salt
- 1/2 teaspoon cayenne pepper
- 1/2 teaspoon paprika
- 1/4 teaspoon black pepper
- 1/4 cup green bell pepper, finely chopped
- 1/4 cup red bell pepper, finely chopped
- 1/4 cup onion, finely chopped
- 2 tablespoons celery, finely chopped
- 2 tablespoons fresh parsley, chopped
- 1 large egg, beaten
- 1/2 cup milk
- Vegetable oil for frying
- Lemon wedges for serving
- Hot pepper sauce or aioli for dipping (optional)

Instructions:

Prepare the Conch:
- Ensure that the conch meat is cleaned and finely chopped. You can tenderize it if needed.

Make the Batter:
- In a large mixing bowl, combine the flour, baking powder, salt, cayenne pepper, paprika, and black pepper.
- Add the finely chopped conch, green bell pepper, red bell pepper, onion, celery, and fresh parsley to the dry ingredients. Mix well to coat the conch and vegetables with the flour mixture.

Create the Fritter Batter:
- In a separate bowl, whisk together the beaten egg and milk.
- Pour the egg and milk mixture into the conch and vegetable mixture. Stir until everything is well combined, creating a thick batter.

Fry the Conch Fritters:

- In a deep skillet or deep fryer, heat vegetable oil to 350°F (180°C).
- Drop spoonfuls of the batter into the hot oil, forming small fritters. Fry until they are golden brown and cooked through, about 3-4 minutes per side.
- Use a slotted spoon to remove the conch fritters from the oil and place them on a plate lined with paper towels to absorb excess oil.

Serve:
- Serve the conch fritters hot, garnished with fresh parsley and lemon wedges.

Optional:
- Serve with hot pepper sauce or aioli on the side for dipping.

Enjoy these Conch Fritters as a delicious appetizer or snack, showcasing the unique flavors of the Caribbean!

Main Courses:

Jamaican Jerk Chicken: Chicken marinated in a spicy jerk seasoning.

Ingredients:

For the Jerk Marinade:

- 4 lbs (about 1.8 kg) chicken pieces (drumsticks, thighs, or wings)
- 6-8 green onions, chopped
- 4-6 Scotch bonnet peppers, seeds and ribs removed (adjust to your spice preference)
- 1 large onion, chopped
- 4 cloves garlic, minced
- 1 tablespoon fresh ginger, grated
- 3 tablespoons fresh thyme leaves
- 2 tablespoons allspice berries, ground
- 2 teaspoons ground cinnamon
- 2 teaspoons ground nutmeg
- 2 tablespoons brown sugar
- 2 tablespoons soy sauce
- 1/4 cup vegetable oil
- 1/4 cup vinegar (white or apple cider)
- Juice of 2 limes
- Salt and black pepper to taste

Instructions:

Prepare the Jerk Marinade:
- In a blender or food processor, combine green onions, Scotch bonnet peppers, onion, garlic, ginger, thyme, allspice, cinnamon, nutmeg, brown sugar, soy sauce, vegetable oil, vinegar, lime juice, salt, and black pepper. Blend until you have a smooth paste.

Marinate the Chicken:
- Make several deep cuts in the chicken pieces to allow the marinade to penetrate. Place the chicken in a large bowl or a resealable plastic bag.

- Rub the jerk marinade all over the chicken, making sure it gets into the cuts. If possible, let it marinate in the refrigerator for at least 4 hours, or overnight for the best flavor.

Cook the Jerk Chicken:
- Preheat your grill or oven to medium-high heat.
- If grilling, place the chicken on the grill and cook for about 25-30 minutes, turning occasionally, until the chicken is cooked through and has a nice char.
- If baking, preheat your oven to 375°F (190°C). Place the chicken on a baking sheet lined with foil and bake for about 45-50 minutes, or until the chicken is fully cooked.

Rest and Serve:
- Allow the jerk chicken to rest for a few minutes before serving. Garnish with additional fresh thyme or sliced green onions if desired.

Serve with Traditional Sides:
- Serve Jamaican Jerk Chicken with traditional sides like rice and peas, fried plantains, or a fresh tropical salad.

Enjoy the bold and spicy flavors of Jamaican Jerk Chicken! Adjust the spice level to suit your taste preferences.

Curry Goat: Tender goat meat slow-cooked in a flavorful curry sauce.

Ingredients:

- 3 lbs (about 1.4 kg) goat meat, cut into chunks
- 2 large onions, finely chopped
- 4 cloves garlic, minced
- 2 tablespoons curry powder
- 1 teaspoon ground turmeric
- 1 teaspoon ground cumin
- 1 teaspoon ground coriander
- 1 teaspoon chili powder (adjust to taste)
- 2 teaspoons thyme, dried
- 2 bay leaves
- 2-3 Scotch bonnet peppers, seeds and ribs removed (wear gloves when handling)
- 2 tablespoons vegetable oil
- 2 cups coconut milk
- 2 cups chicken or vegetable broth
- Salt and black pepper to taste
- Fresh cilantro or parsley for garnish (optional)
- Lime wedges for serving

Instructions:

Marinate the Goat Meat:
- In a large bowl, season the goat meat with salt, black pepper, and half of the minced garlic. Let it marinate for at least 30 minutes or overnight in the refrigerator for better flavor.

Prepare the Curry Paste:
- In a blender or food processor, combine the chopped onions, remaining garlic, curry powder, ground turmeric, ground cumin, ground coriander, chili powder, thyme, Scotch bonnet peppers, and vegetable oil. Blend until you have a smooth paste.

Cook the Curry Goat:
- In a large, heavy-bottomed pot, heat a bit of oil over medium-high heat. Add the marinated goat meat and brown on all sides.
- Add the curry paste to the pot and stir well, coating the meat in the curry mixture.

- Pour in the coconut milk and chicken or vegetable broth. Add bay leaves, and bring the mixture to a boil.
- Reduce the heat to low, cover the pot, and let it simmer for 2 to 2.5 hours, or until the goat meat is tender. Stir occasionally, and add more broth or water if needed.

Adjust Seasoning and Serve:
- Adjust salt and pepper to taste. If you prefer a thicker sauce, you can simmer uncovered for a bit longer until the sauce thickens.
- Garnish with fresh cilantro or parsley if desired.

Serve with Rice:
- Serve the Curry Goat over steamed rice or with your favorite Caribbean side dishes. Don't forget lime wedges on the side for squeezing over the meat.

Enjoy the savory and aromatic flavors of this Caribbean Curry Goat!

Roti: Flatbread with various fillings like curried chicken, shrimp, or vegetables.

Ingredients:

For the Roti Dough:

- 3 cups all-purpose flour
- 1 teaspoon salt
- 1 cup water (or as needed)
- 2 tablespoons vegetable oil

For the Filling:

- Your choice of curried chicken, shrimp, or vegetables (see separate recipes below)

Instructions:

For the Roti Dough:

Prepare the Dough:
- In a large mixing bowl, combine the all-purpose flour and salt. Gradually add water and mix until a soft, smooth dough forms. You may need more or less water depending on the flour.
- Knead the dough on a floured surface for about 5-7 minutes until it becomes elastic.
- Divide the dough into golf ball-sized portions.
- Coat each ball with a bit of vegetable oil, place them on a tray, cover with a cloth, and let them rest for at least 30 minutes.

Roll Out the Roti:
- Take one dough ball and roll it out into a thin, flat disc on a floured surface. Aim for a thickness of about 1/16 to 1/8 inch.
- Brush the surface with a little vegetable oil.
- Fold the rolled-out dough into a square or rectangle, making sure to trap air inside the layers.
- Heat a griddle or flat pan over medium-high heat.

- Cook each roti on the hot griddle for about 1-2 minutes on each side or until it puffs up and develops golden brown spots.
- Remove from the griddle and keep warm.

For the Filling:

Curried Chicken:

- Cook boneless, skinless chicken pieces in a flavorful curry sauce made with onions, garlic, ginger, curry powder, thyme, and coconut milk.

Curried Shrimp:

- Sauté shrimp in a curry sauce with garlic, ginger, onions, curry powder, coconut milk, and a touch of lime juice.

Vegetable Filling:

- Sauté a mix of your favorite vegetables such as potatoes, carrots, peas, and spinach in a curry sauce made with onions, garlic, ginger, and spices.

Assemble the Roti:

Place a portion of your chosen filling in the center of each roti.
Fold the sides over the filling to form a rectangular or square packet.
Serve the filled roti warm and enjoy!

Roti can be enjoyed on its own or with chutney on the side. It's a satisfying and flavorful dish that showcases the diverse and delicious flavors of the Caribbean.

Bahamian Rock Lobster Tail: Grilled or baked lobster tail with island spices.

Ingredients:

- 4 lobster tails, thawed if frozen
- 1/4 cup olive oil
- 3 tablespoons fresh lime juice
- 2 teaspoons paprika
- 1 teaspoon garlic powder
- 1 teaspoon onion powder
- 1 teaspoon dried thyme
- 1/2 teaspoon ground allspice
- 1/2 teaspoon cayenne pepper (adjust to taste)
- Salt and black pepper to taste
- Fresh parsley, chopped, for garnish
- Lime wedges for serving

Instructions:

Prepare the Lobster Tails:
- Preheat your grill to medium-high heat or preheat your oven to 400°F (200°C).
- Using kitchen shears, cut the top of the lobster shell lengthwise down the center, stopping at the tail. Carefully loosen the meat from the shell, keeping it attached at the base.
- Lift the lobster meat and lay it on top of the shell, exposing it. This is known as "butterflying."

Prepare the Marinade:
- In a bowl, whisk together olive oil, fresh lime juice, paprika, garlic powder, onion powder, dried thyme, ground allspice, cayenne pepper, salt, and black pepper.

Marinate the Lobster Tails:
- Brush the lobster tails generously with the marinade, making sure to coat the meat and the shell.
- Allow the lobster tails to marinate for at least 15-30 minutes to let the flavors infuse.

Grill or Bake the Lobster Tails:

- If Grilling: Place the lobster tails on the preheated grill, shell side down. Grill for about 5-7 minutes until the meat is opaque and cooked through, basting with the marinade occasionally.
- If Baking: Place the lobster tails on a baking sheet lined with foil. Bake in the preheated oven for about 12-15 minutes or until the meat is opaque and cooked through, basting with the marinade occasionally.

Garnish and Serve:
- Once cooked, sprinkle chopped fresh parsley over the lobster tails for garnish.
- Serve the Bahamian Rock Lobster Tails with lime wedges on the side for an extra burst of citrus flavor.

This flavorful Bahamian Rock Lobster Tail dish is a perfect showcase of the Caribbean's rich seafood offerings. Enjoy it with your favorite side dishes for a complete and delicious meal!

Ackee and Saltfish: Jamaica's national dish featuring ackee fruit and salted cod.

Ingredients:

- 1 lb (about 450g) salted codfish
- 2 cans (about 2 cups) canned ackee, drained and rinsed
- 2 tablespoons vegetable oil
- 1 medium onion, thinly sliced
- 1 bell pepper (any color), thinly sliced
- 2 cloves garlic, minced
- 1-2 Scotch bonnet peppers, seeds and ribs removed (optional, for heat)
- 2 sprigs thyme
- 1 medium tomato, diced
- Salt and black pepper to taste
- Green onions, chopped, for garnish
- Fried dumplings or boiled green bananas, for serving (optional)
- Rice and peas, for serving (optional)

Instructions:

Prepare the Salted Cod:
- Rinse the salted cod under cold running water to remove excess salt.
- Place the cod in a bowl of cold water and let it soak for 1-2 hours, changing the water a few times. This will help to further reduce the saltiness.
- Once soaked, flake the cod into small pieces, removing any bones and skin.

Cook the Ackee and Saltfish:
- Heat vegetable oil in a large skillet over medium heat.
- Add sliced onions, bell pepper, minced garlic, and Scotch bonnet peppers (if using). Sauté until the vegetables are softened.
- Add the flaked salted cod to the skillet. Stir well to combine with the vegetables.
- Add the drained and rinsed ackee to the skillet. Gently fold in the ackee, being careful not to break it up too much.
- Add thyme sprigs and diced tomatoes. Continue to cook for a few minutes until the ackee is heated through.
- Season with salt and black pepper to taste. Be mindful of the salt, as the cod may still have some residual saltiness.

- Remove the thyme sprigs before serving.

Serve:
- Garnish with chopped green onions.
- Ackee and Saltfish can be served with fried dumplings, boiled green bananas, or rice and peas.
- Enjoy this delicious and iconic Jamaican dish!

Ackee and Saltfish is often enjoyed as a hearty breakfast or brunch dish, but it can be served at any time of the day. It offers a delightful combination of flavors and textures, showcasing the unique taste of ackee and the savory notes of salted cod.

Pelau: One-pot rice dish with meat, rice, and pigeon peas.

Ingredients:

- 2 lbs chicken pieces (thighs, drumsticks, or a mix)
- 2 cups parboiled rice
- 1 cup pigeon peas (fresh, frozen, or canned)
- 1 large onion, finely chopped
- 2 cloves garlic, minced
- 1 bell pepper (any color), diced
- 1 medium carrot, diced
- 2 tablespoons vegetable oil
- 2 tablespoons brown sugar
- 2 tablespoons dark soy sauce
- 1 tablespoon Worcestershire sauce
- 1 teaspoon thyme, dried
- 2 sprigs thyme (for garnish)
- 2 cups coconut milk
- 3 cups chicken broth
- Salt and black pepper to taste
- Scotch bonnet pepper (optional, for heat)

Instructions:

Prepare the Chicken:
- Season the chicken pieces with salt, black pepper, and minced garlic. Let them marinate for at least 30 minutes.

Brown the Chicken:
- In a large, heavy-bottomed pot or Dutch oven, heat vegetable oil over medium-high heat.
- Sprinkle brown sugar over the chicken pieces and add them to the pot. Brown the chicken on all sides until it gets a nice caramelized color.

Add Vegetables and Aromatics:
- Add chopped onions, diced bell pepper, and diced carrots to the pot. Sauté until the vegetables are softened.
- Stir in thyme (dried) and minced garlic. If you want some heat, add a whole Scotch bonnet pepper (remember to pierce it with a knife for flavor without excessive heat).

Add Rice and Pigeon Peas:
- Add parboiled rice and pigeon peas to the pot. Mix well to coat them with the flavorful ingredients.

Pour in Coconut Milk and Broth:
- Pour in coconut milk, dark soy sauce, and Worcestershire sauce. Stir to combine.
- Add chicken broth to the pot, ensuring that the liquid covers the rice and chicken. Adjust the salt and pepper to taste.

Simmer and Cook:
- Bring the pot to a boil, then reduce the heat to low. Cover and let it simmer for about 25-30 minutes or until the rice is cooked and the liquid is absorbed.

Garnish and Serve:
- Garnish the Pelau with fresh thyme sprigs.
- Serve the Pelau hot, fluffing the rice with a fork before serving.

Pelau is a comforting and flavorful dish, and it's often enjoyed during social gatherings and celebrations in the Caribbean. It's a complete meal in one pot, making it convenient and delicious.

Bajan Flying Fish Cou-Cou: Cornmeal and okra dish with flying fish.

Ingredients:

For the Cou-Cou:

- 1 cup cornmeal
- 2 cups water
- 1 cup okra, finely chopped
- 1 onion, finely chopped
- 2 cloves garlic, minced
- 1 sprig thyme
- 2 cups chicken or vegetable broth
- Salt and pepper to taste

For the Flying Fish:

- 4-6 flying fish fillets (substitute with another fish if flying fish is not available)
- 1 lime, juiced
- Salt and pepper to taste
- 2 tablespoons vegetable oil

For the Sauce:

- 1 onion, finely sliced
- 1 bell pepper (any color), thinly sliced
- 1 tomato, diced
- 2 cloves garlic, minced
- 1 cup coconut milk
- 1 tablespoon Bajan hot sauce (adjust to taste)
- Salt and pepper to taste

Instructions:

For the Flying Fish:

Marinate the Fish:

- Rinse the flying fish fillets and pat them dry.
- Season the fillets with salt, pepper, and lime juice. Let them marinate for about 30 minutes.

Cook the Fish:
- Heat vegetable oil in a skillet over medium heat.
- Pan-sear the fish fillets for about 3-4 minutes on each side or until they are cooked through and have a golden-brown crust.
- Remove the fish from the skillet and set aside.

For the Cou-Cou:

Prepare the Okra:
- In a food processor, blend the okra until it becomes a slimy consistency. Set aside.

Cook the Cou-Cou:
- In a pot, bring 2 cups of water to a boil.
- In a separate bowl, mix the cornmeal with enough cold water to form a smooth paste.
- Gradually whisk the cornmeal paste into the boiling water, stirring continuously to avoid lumps.
- Add chopped onion, minced garlic, chopped okra, thyme, and chicken or vegetable broth. Continue stirring.
- Reduce the heat to low, cover the pot, and let it simmer for about 20-25 minutes, stirring occasionally, until the cou-cou is smooth and has a thick consistency.
- Season with salt and pepper to taste.

For the Sauce:

Prepare the Vegetables:
- In a separate skillet, heat a bit of oil over medium heat.
- Sauté sliced onion, sliced bell pepper, diced tomato, and minced garlic until the vegetables are softened.

Finish the Sauce:
- Pour in coconut milk and Bajan hot sauce. Stir well.
- Add the pan-seared fish fillets to the sauce. Simmer for a few minutes until the fish is heated through.
- Season the sauce with salt and pepper to taste.

Serve:

- Plate the Cou-Cou:
  - Spoon portions of the cou-cou onto plates or a serving platter.
- Top with Fish and Sauce:
  - Place the pan-seared fish fillets on top of the cou-cou.
  - Pour the sauce with vegetables over the fish.
- Garnish and Enjoy:
  - Garnish with fresh herbs or additional hot sauce if desired.

Bajan Flying Fish Cou-Cou is a flavorful and unique dish that represents the culinary traditions of Barbados. Enjoy this delightful combination of cornmeal, okra, and flying fish with a rich coconut and vegetable sauce.

Guyanese Pepper Pot: Cassava soup with meat and spices.

Ingredients:

- 2 lbs beef or a mix of beef and pork, cut into bite-sized pieces
- 1 cup cassareep (a traditional Guyanese sauce made from cassava)
- 1 large onion, chopped
- 4 cloves garlic, minced
- 1 inch ginger, grated
- 2 wiri wiri peppers or Scotch bonnet peppers, seeds and ribs removed (for less heat, adjust to taste)
- 4 cups water
- 4 cinnamon leaves or bay leaves
- Salt to taste
- 4-5 cups diced cassava
- 1 cup eddoes, peeled and diced (optional)
- 1 cup spinach or callaloo, chopped (optional)

Instructions:

Prepare the Meat:
- In a large pot, brown the meat pieces over medium heat.
- Add chopped onions, minced garlic, grated ginger, and chopped peppers. Sauté until the onions are softened.

Cook the Pepper Pot:
- Pour in cassareep and water, stirring to combine.
- Add cinnamon leaves or bay leaves and season with salt.
- Cover the pot and let it simmer over low heat for 2-3 hours, allowing the meat to become tender and the flavors to meld.

Add Cassava and Greens:
- Add diced cassava and eddoes (if using) to the pot. Simmer until the cassava is tender.
- If desired, add chopped spinach or callaloo in the last 10-15 minutes of cooking.

Serve:
- Remove cinnamon leaves or bay leaves before serving.
- Pepper Pot is traditionally served with rice or traditional Guyanese bread.

Enjoy this flavorful and comforting Guyanese Pepper Pot! The combination of cassareep, spices, and cassava creates a unique and delicious dish that is perfect for warming up on a cool day.

Stewed Conch: Conch cooked in a savory tomato-based sauce.

Ingredients:

- 1 lb conch, cleaned and sliced into bite-sized pieces
- 2 tablespoons vegetable oil
- 1 large onion, finely chopped
- 3 cloves garlic, minced
- 1 bell pepper (any color), diced
- 1 carrot, diced
- 1 celery stalk, diced
- 1 can (14 oz) diced tomatoes
- 1/2 cup tomato sauce
- 1 cup fish or vegetable broth
- 1 teaspoon dried thyme
- 1 teaspoon paprika
- 1/2 teaspoon cayenne pepper (adjust to taste)
- Salt and black pepper to taste
- Fresh parsley, chopped, for garnish
- Cooked rice or crusty bread, for serving

Instructions:

Prepare the Conch:
- If using fresh conch, clean and slice it into bite-sized pieces. If using frozen conch, ensure it is thawed according to package instructions.

Cook the Stewed Conch:
- In a large pot or Dutch oven, heat vegetable oil over medium heat.
- Add chopped onions, minced garlic, diced bell pepper, diced carrot, and diced celery. Sauté until the vegetables are softened.
- Add the sliced conch to the pot and cook for a few minutes until it starts to turn opaque.
- Pour in diced tomatoes, tomato sauce, and fish or vegetable broth. Stir well to combine.
- Season with dried thyme, paprika, cayenne pepper, salt, and black pepper. Adjust the seasoning to your taste preference.
- Bring the mixture to a simmer, then reduce the heat to low, cover, and let it cook for about 30-40 minutes or until the conch is tender.

Garnish and Serve:

- Garnish the Stewed Conch with chopped fresh parsley.
- Serve the Stewed Conch over cooked rice or with crusty bread to soak up the flavorful sauce.

Enjoy this delicious and savory Stewed Conch! The combination of tomatoes, spices, and tender conch creates a dish that is both comforting and bursting with Caribbean flavors.

Vegetarian and Vegan Delights:

Vegan Callaloo: Leafy greens stewed with coconut milk.

Ingredients:

- 1 bunch callaloo (substitute with spinach or Swiss chard if callaloo is unavailable)
- 1 can (14 oz) coconut milk
- 1 onion, finely chopped
- 3 cloves garlic, minced
- 1 bell pepper (any color), diced
- 1 medium tomato, diced
- 1 scallion, chopped
- 1 sprig thyme
- 1 Scotch bonnet pepper, seeds and ribs removed (for less heat, adjust to taste)
- 2 tablespoons vegetable oil
- Salt and black pepper to taste
- Lime wedges for serving

Instructions:

Prepare the Callaloo:
- Wash the callaloo leaves thoroughly. Remove tough stems and chop the leaves.

Cook the Vegan Callaloo:
- In a large pot or Dutch oven, heat vegetable oil over medium heat.
- Add chopped onions, minced garlic, diced bell pepper, and diced tomato. Sauté until the vegetables are softened.
- Pour in coconut milk and stir well to combine.
- Add the chopped callaloo leaves to the pot. Stir and allow the leaves to wilt into the coconut milk mixture.
- Add scallions, thyme, and the Scotch bonnet pepper (whole or pierced for flavor without excessive heat). Adjust the salt and black pepper to taste.
- Cover the pot and let the Vegan Callaloo simmer over low heat for about 15-20 minutes, allowing the flavors to meld.

Serve:
- Discard the Scotch bonnet pepper and thyme sprig before serving.

- Serve the Vegan Callaloo hot, accompanied by rice or your favorite Caribbean side dishes.

Optional:
- Squeeze fresh lime juice over the Vegan Callaloo before serving for an extra burst of citrus flavor.

Enjoy this Vegan Callaloo as a nutritious and flavorful addition to your plant-based meals. It's a classic Caribbean dish that celebrates the vibrant flavors of coconut milk and leafy greens.

Vegetarian Roti: Flatbread with flavorful vegetable fillings.

Ingredients:

For the Roti Dough:

- 3 cups all-purpose flour
- 1 teaspoon salt
- 1 cup water (or as needed)
- 2 tablespoons vegetable oil

For the Vegetable Filling:

- 2 tablespoons vegetable oil
- 1 large onion, thinly sliced
- 2 cloves garlic, minced
- 1 bell pepper (any color), thinly sliced
- 1 medium carrot, julienned
- 1 zucchini, diced
- 1 cup cauliflower florets
- 1 cup spinach, chopped
- 1 teaspoon ground cumin
- 1 teaspoon ground coriander
- 1 teaspoon garam masala
- Salt and black pepper to taste
- Fresh cilantro, chopped, for garnish

Instructions:

For the Roti Dough:

   Prepare the Dough:
   - In a large mixing bowl, combine the all-purpose flour and salt. Gradually add water and mix until a soft, smooth dough forms. You may need more or less water depending on the flour.
   - Knead the dough on a floured surface for about 5-7 minutes until it becomes elastic.

- Divide the dough into golf ball-sized portions.
- Coat each ball with a bit of vegetable oil, place them on a tray, cover with a cloth, and let them rest for at least 30 minutes.

Roll Out the Roti:
- Take one dough ball and roll it out into a thin, flat disc on a floured surface. Aim for a thickness of about 1/16 to 1/8 inch.
- Brush the surface with a little vegetable oil.
- Fold the rolled-out dough into a square or rectangle, making sure to trap air inside the layers.
- Heat a griddle or flat pan over medium-high heat.
- Cook each roti on the hot griddle for about 1-2 minutes on each side or until it puffs up and develops golden brown spots.
- Remove from the griddle and keep warm.

For the Vegetable Filling:

Prepare the Vegetables:
- In a large pan or wok, heat vegetable oil over medium heat.
- Add sliced onions, minced garlic, and julienned carrots. Sauté until the onions are translucent.
- Add diced bell pepper, diced zucchini, cauliflower florets, and continue to sauté until the vegetables are tender yet still crisp.

Season the Filling:
- Sprinkle ground cumin, ground coriander, and garam masala over the vegetables. Stir well to coat.
- Add chopped spinach and cook until wilted.
- Season with salt and black pepper to taste. Adjust the seasoning according to your preference.

Assemble the Vegetarian Roti:
- Place a portion of the vegetable filling in the center of each roti.
- Fold the sides over the filling to form a rectangular or square packet.

Serve:
- Serve the filled Vegetarian Roti warm and garnish with fresh chopped cilantro.

Enjoy these flavorful Vegetarian Rotis, filled with a medley of delicious vegetables! They make for a satisfying and delicious meal.

Rasta Pasta: Pasta dish with a creamy coconut milk sauce and veggies.

Ingredients:

- 8 oz (about 225g) penne or your favorite pasta
- 1 tablespoon vegetable oil
- 1 small onion, finely chopped
- 3 cloves garlic, minced
- 1 bell pepper (any color), thinly sliced
- 1 cup cherry tomatoes, halved
- 1 cup broccoli florets
- 1 cup sliced mushrooms
- 1 can (14 oz) coconut milk
- 1 teaspoon dried thyme
- 1 teaspoon paprika
- 1/2 teaspoon cayenne pepper (adjust to taste)
- Salt and black pepper to taste
- 1/2 cup grated Parmesan or nutritional yeast for a vegan option
- Fresh parsley, chopped, for garnish

Instructions:

Cook the Pasta:
- Cook the pasta according to the package instructions. Drain and set aside.

Prepare the Vegetables:
- In a large pan, heat vegetable oil over medium heat.
- Add finely chopped onion and minced garlic. Sauté until the onions are translucent.
- Add thinly sliced bell pepper, halved cherry tomatoes, broccoli florets, and sliced mushrooms. Cook until the vegetables are slightly tender but still vibrant.

Make the Coconut Milk Sauce:
- Pour in the coconut milk and stir well to combine.
- Season the sauce with dried thyme, paprika, cayenne pepper, salt, and black pepper. Adjust the seasoning according to your taste.

Combine Pasta and Sauce:
- Add the cooked pasta to the pan with the coconut milk sauce and vegetables.

- Toss everything together until the pasta is well coated in the creamy sauce.

Finish and Serve:
- Stir in grated Parmesan cheese or nutritional yeast for a vegan option. Mix until the cheese is melted and the sauce is creamy.
- Garnish with chopped fresh parsley.
- Serve the Rasta Pasta hot, and enjoy the vibrant flavors of this coconut-infused pasta dish!

Rasta Pasta is a delicious and colorful dish that combines the creaminess of coconut milk with a variety of veggies, creating a satisfying and flavorful meal. Feel free to customize the vegetables to suit your preferences and add some Jamaican jerk seasoning for an extra Caribbean kick!

Trinidadian Aloo Pie: Fried or baked potato pies with spiced fillings.

Ingredients:

For the Dough:

- 2 cups all-purpose flour
- 1/2 teaspoon salt
- 2 tablespoons vegetable oil
- Water (as needed to form a dough)

For the Filling:

- 2 large potatoes, boiled and mashed
- 1 tablespoon vegetable oil
- 1 small onion, finely chopped
- 2 cloves garlic, minced
- 1 teaspoon curry powder
- 1/2 teaspoon ground cumin
- 1/2 teaspoon ground coriander
- 1/2 teaspoon ground turmeric
- Salt and black pepper to taste
- Hot pepper sauce or chopped hot pepper (optional, for heat)
- Chopped cilantro or parsley for garnish

For Frying:

- Vegetable oil for deep frying

Instructions:

For the Dough:

    Prepare the Dough:
- In a bowl, combine the all-purpose flour and salt.
- Add the vegetable oil and gradually add water while kneading until a soft, non-sticky dough forms.
- Cover the dough with a damp cloth and let it rest for about 30 minutes.

For the Filling:

Prepare the Filling:
- In a pan, heat vegetable oil over medium heat.
- Add chopped onions and minced garlic. Sauté until the onions are translucent.
- Add curry powder, ground cumin, ground coriander, and ground turmeric. Stir well to combine.
- Add the mashed potatoes and continue to cook, stirring, until the mixture is well-spiced and heated through.
- Season with salt, black pepper, and hot pepper sauce or chopped hot pepper (if using). Adjust the seasoning to your taste.
- Remove from heat and let the filling cool.

Assembling and Frying:

Roll and Fill the Dough:
- Divide the rested dough into golf ball-sized portions.
- Roll each portion into a small disc, like a mini-tortilla.
- Place a spoonful of the cooled potato filling in the center of each disc.
- Fold the edges of the disc over the filling, creating a half-moon shape, and seal the edges by pressing with a fork.

Fry the Aloo Pies:
- In a deep pan or fryer, heat vegetable oil for deep frying over medium-high heat.
- Carefully place the aloo pies into the hot oil, a few at a time, and fry until they are golden brown on both sides.
- Remove the fried aloo pies and drain them on paper towels to remove excess oil.

Serve:
- Garnish the Trinidadian Aloo Pies with chopped cilantro or parsley.
- Serve the aloo pies hot as a delicious snack or appetizer.

Enjoy these Trinidadian Aloo Pies, filled with spiced potatoes and encased in a golden, crispy shell! They are perfect for snacking or as a tasty addition to your Trinidadian culinary repertoire.

Jamaican Ital Stew: Vegan stew with vegetables and coconut milk.

Ingredients:

- 1 cup dried red kidney beans, soaked overnight (or use canned beans for a quicker option)
- 2 tablespoons coconut oil
- 1 large onion, chopped
- 3 cloves garlic, minced
- 1 bell pepper (any color), diced
- 2 carrots, peeled and diced
- 2 medium potatoes, peeled and diced
- 1 cup pumpkin or butternut squash, peeled and diced
- 1 zucchini, diced
- 1 can (14 oz) coconut milk
- 2 cups vegetable broth
- 2 sprigs thyme
- 2 scallions, chopped
- 1 teaspoon ground allspice
- 1 teaspoon ground coriander
- 1 teaspoon curry powder
- Salt and black pepper to taste
- Scotch bonnet pepper (whole or pierced, for flavor without excessive heat)
- Fresh parsley or cilantro, chopped, for garnish
- Cooked rice or Jamaican rice and peas, for serving

Instructions:

Prepare the Beans:
- If using dried kidney beans, soak them overnight. Rinse and drain before using.
- If using canned beans, rinse and drain them.

Cook the Ital Stew:
- In a large pot, heat coconut oil over medium heat.
- Add chopped onions and minced garlic. Sauté until the onions are translucent.
- Add diced bell pepper, carrots, potatoes, pumpkin or squash, and zucchini. Stir well to coat the vegetables in the coconut oil.
- Pour in coconut milk and vegetable broth. Stir to combine.

- Add soaked (or canned) kidney beans to the pot.
- Season the stew with thyme, scallions, ground allspice, ground coriander, curry powder, salt, and black pepper. Add the whole Scotch bonnet pepper.
- Bring the stew to a boil, then reduce the heat to low, cover, and let it simmer for about 30-40 minutes or until the vegetables and beans are tender.

Adjust Seasoning and Serve:
- Taste the Ital Stew and adjust the seasoning if necessary.
- Remove the whole Scotch bonnet pepper before serving.

Serve:
- Serve the Jamaican Ital Stew over cooked rice or Jamaican rice and peas.
- Garnish with chopped fresh parsley or cilantro.

Enjoy this Jamaican Ital Stew for a taste of the Caribbean with its rich coconut flavors and vibrant spices. It's a wholesome and satisfying vegan dish that's perfect for a comforting meal.

Seafood Specialities:

Grilled Caribbean Spiny Lobster: Lobster grilled with Caribbean spices.

Ingredients:

- 2 Caribbean spiny lobsters (or any lobster variety available), split in half
- 1/2 cup olive oil
- 3 tablespoons fresh lime juice
- 2 tablespoons fresh orange juice
- 3 cloves garlic, minced
- 1 teaspoon ground cumin
- 1 teaspoon paprika
- 1 teaspoon dried thyme
- 1 teaspoon cayenne pepper (adjust to taste)
- Salt and black pepper to taste
- Fresh parsley or cilantro, chopped, for garnish
- Lime wedges for serving

Instructions:

Prepare the Marinade:
- In a bowl, whisk together olive oil, fresh lime juice, fresh orange juice, minced garlic, ground cumin, paprika, dried thyme, cayenne pepper, salt, and black pepper.

Marinate the Lobster:
- Place the split lobster halves in a shallow dish.
- Pour the marinade over the lobster, ensuring each piece is well-coated. Use a brush to distribute the marinade evenly.
- Cover the dish and let the lobster marinate in the refrigerator for at least 30 minutes, allowing the flavors to infuse.

Preheat the Grill:
- Preheat your grill to medium-high heat.

Grill the Lobster:
- Place the marinated lobster halves on the preheated grill, flesh side down.
- Grill for about 5-7 minutes, basting with the remaining marinade, until the lobster meat is opaque and has grill marks.
- Flip the lobster halves and grill for an additional 5-7 minutes or until fully cooked.

Serve:
- Transfer the grilled lobster to a serving platter.
- Garnish with chopped fresh parsley or cilantro.
- Serve the Grilled Caribbean Spiny Lobster hot, accompanied by lime wedges for an extra burst of citrus flavor.

Enjoy this delightful seafood specialty with the essence of Caribbean spices, providing a unique and savory experience. It's a perfect dish for a special occasion or a taste of the tropics right at home.

Jamaican Brown Stew Fish: Fish marinated and stewed in a rich, brown sauce.

Ingredients:

- 4 fish fillets (snapper, grouper, or your preferred white fish)
- 1 cup all-purpose flour (for coating)
- 2 tablespoons vegetable oil
- 1 large onion, thinly sliced
- 2 bell peppers (any color), thinly sliced
- 3 cloves garlic, minced
- 1 medium carrot, julienned
- 2 tomatoes, chopped
- 2 tablespoons ketchup
- 2 tablespoons soy sauce
- 1 tablespoon brown sugar
- 1 teaspoon dried thyme
- 1 teaspoon allspice
- 1 teaspoon paprika
- 1 scallion, chopped
- 2 cups vegetable or fish broth
- Salt and black pepper to taste
- Fresh parsley, chopped, for garnish
- Lime wedges for serving

Instructions:

Prepare the Fish:
- Rinse the fish fillets and pat them dry with paper towels.
- Season the fish with salt and black pepper.
- Coat each fillet with all-purpose flour, shaking off any excess.

Brown the Fish:
- In a large skillet or frying pan, heat vegetable oil over medium-high heat.
- Brown the fish fillets on both sides until they have a golden crust. This step is to give the fish a nice sear but it doesn't need to be fully cooked at this point.
- Once browned, remove the fish fillets from the skillet and set them aside.

Prepare the Stew:
- In the same skillet, add a bit more oil if needed.

- Add sliced onions, bell peppers, minced garlic, and julienned carrots. Sauté until the vegetables are softened.
- Stir in chopped tomatoes, ketchup, soy sauce, brown sugar, dried thyme, allspice, paprika, and chopped scallion. Mix well.
- Pour in vegetable or fish broth, stirring to combine. Bring the mixture to a simmer.

Stew the Fish:
- Carefully place the browned fish fillets back into the skillet, making sure they are submerged in the stew.
- Cover the skillet and let the fish stew in the sauce for about 15-20 minutes or until the fish is cooked through.
- Adjust the seasoning with salt and black pepper to taste.

Serve:
- Garnish the Jamaican Brown Stew Fish with chopped fresh parsley.
- Serve hot, accompanied by lime wedges for squeezing over the fish.

Enjoy this flavorful and comforting Jamaican Brown Stew Fish with its rich brown sauce and aromatic spices. It pairs well with rice and peas or your favorite side dishes for a complete and satisfying meal.

Belizean Ceviche: Fresh seafood cured in citrus juices.

Ingredients:

- 1 lb fresh conch or shrimp, cleaned and diced into small pieces
- 1 cup fresh lime juice
- 1/2 cup fresh orange juice
- 1 medium red onion, finely chopped
- 1 bell pepper (any color), finely chopped
- 2 tomatoes, diced
- 1 cucumber, peeled and diced
- 1 jalapeño or habanero pepper, finely chopped (adjust to taste)
- 1/2 cup chopped fresh cilantro
- Salt and black pepper to taste
- Tortilla chips or plantain chips for serving

Instructions:

Prepare the Seafood:
- If using conch, ensure it is cleaned and diced into small pieces. If using shrimp, peel, devein, and chop into bite-sized pieces.

Marinate the Seafood:
- In a non-reactive bowl, combine the diced seafood with fresh lime juice and fresh orange juice.
- Make sure the seafood is fully submerged in the citrus juices. Cover the bowl and refrigerate for at least 2 hours or until the seafood turns opaque and "cooked" in the acid.

Combine Ingredients:
- After marinating, drain most of the citrus juices, leaving a small amount for flavor.
- Add finely chopped red onion, bell pepper, tomatoes, cucumber, jalapeño or habanero pepper, and chopped cilantro to the seafood. Mix well.

Season:
- Season the ceviche with salt and black pepper to taste. Adjust the seasoning according to your preference.

Chill:
- Return the ceviche to the refrigerator and let it chill for an additional 30 minutes to allow the flavors to meld.

Serve:
- Serve the Belizean Ceviche in individual bowls or on a platter.
- Accompany the ceviche with tortilla chips or plantain chips for scooping.

Enjoy this refreshing and citrus-infused Belizean Ceviche as a delightful appetizer or light meal. The combination of fresh seafood and vibrant vegetables creates a dish that is perfect for warm weather and tropical vibes.

Curried Crab and Dumplings: Crab cooked in a curry sauce with dumplings.

Ingredients:

For the Curry Crab:

- 2 lbs crab, cleaned and cracked
- 2 tablespoons curry powder
- 1 onion, finely chopped
- 3 cloves garlic, minced
- 1 bell pepper (any color), chopped
- 1 tomato, diced
- 1 scallion, chopped
- 1 sprig thyme
- 2 tablespoons vegetable oil
- 1 cup coconut milk
- 1 cup seafood or vegetable broth
- Salt and black pepper to taste
- Scotch bonnet pepper or hot pepper sauce (optional, for heat)
- Fresh cilantro or parsley, chopped, for garnish

For the Dumplings:

- 2 cups all-purpose flour
- 1 teaspoon baking powder
- 1/2 teaspoon salt
- Water (as needed to form a dough)

Instructions:

For the Curry Crab:

Prepare the Crab:
- Clean and crack the crab into manageable pieces.

Make the Curry Sauce:
- In a large pot or Dutch oven, heat vegetable oil over medium heat.

- Add chopped onions, minced garlic, and curry powder. Sauté until the onions are translucent and the curry is aromatic.
- Add chopped bell pepper, diced tomato, scallion, and thyme. Cook until the vegetables are softened.
- Add cleaned and cracked crab to the pot. Stir to coat the crab in the curry mixture.
- Pour in coconut milk and seafood or vegetable broth. Season with salt and black pepper. Add Scotch bonnet pepper or hot pepper sauce for heat, if desired.
- Bring the curry crab to a simmer, cover the pot, and let it cook for about 20-25 minutes or until the crab is fully cooked and the flavors have melded.

Prepare Dumplings:
- In a bowl, combine all-purpose flour, baking powder, and salt.
- Gradually add water and knead to form a soft, non-sticky dough.
- Divide the dough into small portions and shape them into dumplings.

Add Dumplings to Curry:
- Carefully drop the dumplings into the simmering curry crab. Cover the pot and let them cook for about 10-15 minutes or until the dumplings are cooked through.

Serve:
- Garnish the Curried Crab and Dumplings with chopped fresh cilantro or parsley.
- Serve hot, with additional hot pepper sauce on the side for those who enjoy extra heat.

Enjoy this delicious and hearty Caribbean dish of Curried Crab and Dumplings, where the aromatic curry sauce enhances the flavors of the crab, and the dumplings add a comforting element to the meal.

Dominican Mangu with Shrimp: Mashed plantains with seasoned shrimp.

Ingredients:

For the Mangu (Mashed Plantains):

- 4 ripe plantains, peeled and cut into chunks
- 1/4 cup butter or olive oil
- 1/4 cup milk (optional)
- Salt to taste

For the Seasoned Shrimp:

- 1 lb shrimp, peeled and deveined
- 2 tablespoons olive oil
- 3 cloves garlic, minced
- 1 teaspoon dried oregano
- 1 teaspoon ground cumin
- 1 teaspoon paprika
- Salt and black pepper to taste
- Fresh cilantro or parsley, chopped, for garnish

Instructions:

For the Mangu (Mashed Plantains):

Boil the Plantains:
- In a large pot, bring water to a boil. Add the plantain chunks and cook until they are tender, about 10-15 minutes.

Mash the Plantains:
- Drain the plantains and place them in a bowl.
- Add butter or olive oil, and optionally, milk for creaminess.
- Mash the plantains until smooth and well combined. Season with salt to taste.

For the Seasoned Shrimp:

Prepare the Shrimp:
- In a bowl, combine shrimp with minced garlic, dried oregano, ground cumin, paprika, salt, and black pepper. Toss to coat the shrimp evenly.

Sauté the Shrimp:
- In a large skillet, heat olive oil over medium-high heat.
- Add the seasoned shrimp to the skillet and cook until they are pink and opaque, about 2-3 minutes per side.
- Remove the skillet from heat and set aside.

Assemble the Mangu with Shrimp:

Serve:
- Spoon the mashed plantains onto a plate.
- Arrange the seasoned shrimp on top of the mangu.
- Garnish with chopped fresh cilantro or parsley.
- Serve the Dominican Mangu with Shrimp hot and enjoy the delicious combination of creamy mashed plantains and seasoned shrimp.

This dish offers a wonderful blend of textures and flavors, with the sweet and savory mangu complementing the seasoned shrimp. It's a comforting and satisfying meal that reflects the rich culinary traditions of the Dominican Republic.

Side Dishes and Condiments:

Coconut Rice and Peas: Rice cooked with coconut milk and kidney beans.

Ingredients:

- 1 cup long-grain white rice
- 1 can (14 oz) coconut milk
- 1 cup water
- 1 cup cooked kidney beans (canned or cooked from dried beans)
- 1 small onion, finely chopped
- 2 cloves garlic, minced
- 1 sprig thyme
- 1 scallion, chopped
- 1 teaspoon salt (adjust to taste)
- 1/2 teaspoon black pepper
- 1 Scotch bonnet pepper or hot pepper sauce (optional, for heat)
- 2 tablespoons vegetable oil

Instructions:

Prepare the Rice:
- Rinse the rice under cold water until the water runs clear. Drain.

Sauté Aromatics:
- In a large pot or saucepan, heat vegetable oil over medium heat.
- Add finely chopped onion, minced garlic, thyme, and chopped scallion. Sauté until the onions are translucent.

Add Rice and Coconut Milk:
- Add the rinsed rice to the pot and stir to coat the rice in the aromatic mixture.
- Pour in the coconut milk and water. Stir well to combine.

Season and Simmer:
- Add cooked kidney beans to the pot and season with salt and black pepper. Stir to incorporate the ingredients.
- If using Scotch bonnet pepper, add it whole to the pot for flavor. Alternatively, you can pierce the pepper with a fork to release more heat. If you prefer less heat, you can add hot pepper sauce later according to your taste.

- Bring the mixture to a boil, then reduce the heat to low, cover the pot, and let it simmer for 18-20 minutes or until the rice is cooked and has absorbed the liquid.

Fluff and Serve:
- Once the rice is cooked, fluff it with a fork to separate the grains.
- Remove the Scotch bonnet pepper if used whole.

Serve:
- Serve the Coconut Rice and Peas hot as a flavorful side dish.
- Adjust the seasoning if necessary and enjoy this delicious and aromatic Caribbean staple!

Coconut Rice and Peas is a wonderful side dish that pairs well with a variety of main courses, particularly Caribbean and Jamaican dishes. The combination of coconut milk, kidney beans, and aromatic spices makes it a tasty and comforting addition to your meal.

Festival: Sweet fried dough served as a side or snack.

Ingredients:

- 2 cups all-purpose flour
- 1/4 cup cornmeal
- 1/4 cup sugar
- 1 teaspoon baking powder
- 1/4 teaspoon salt
- 2/3 cup water
- 1/4 cup milk
- Vegetable oil for frying

Instructions:

Prepare the Dry Ingredients:
- In a large bowl, whisk together the all-purpose flour, cornmeal, sugar, baking powder, and salt.

Create the Dough:
- Gradually add water and milk to the dry ingredients, stirring continuously to form a smooth dough. Adjust the amount of liquid if needed to achieve a soft and pliable consistency.

Shape the Festival:
- Take small portions of the dough and roll them into cylinders or elongated shapes, about 3-4 inches long. You can shape them as desired, either as small logs or twists.

Heat the Oil:
- In a deep skillet or pot, heat vegetable oil over medium-high heat until it reaches 350-375°F (175-190°C).

Fry the Festival:
- Carefully place the shaped dough into the hot oil, a few at a time, to avoid overcrowding.
- Fry the festival until they are golden brown on all sides, turning occasionally to ensure even cooking. This usually takes about 3-5 minutes.

Drain and Serve:
- Use a slotted spoon to remove the fried festival from the oil, allowing excess oil to drain.
- Place the fried festival on paper towels to absorb any remaining oil.

Serve:
- Serve the festival warm as a delightful side dish or snack.
- Festival is often enjoyed with fried fish, jerk chicken, or other Caribbean dishes.

Enjoy these sweet fried dough delights as a tasty addition to your Caribbean-inspired meals or as a delightful snack on their own!

Callaloo Soup: Leafy green soup with okra and various vegetables.

Ingredients:

- 2 bunches of callaloo or substitute with spinach or Swiss chard, washed and chopped
- 1 cup okra, sliced
- 1 large onion, chopped
- 3 cloves garlic, minced
- 1 large carrot, diced
- 1 medium sweet potato, peeled and diced
- 1 medium yam, peeled and diced
- 1 cup pumpkin or butternut squash, diced
- 1 scallion, chopped
- 1 sprig thyme
- 2 bay leaves
- 1 can (14 oz) coconut milk
- 6 cups vegetable or chicken broth
- 2 tablespoons vegetable oil
- Salt and black pepper to taste
- Scotch bonnet pepper or hot pepper sauce (optional, for heat)
- Lime wedges for serving

Instructions:

Prepare the Vegetables:
- Wash and chop the callaloo or substitute with spinach or Swiss chard.
- Slice the okra, chop the onion, mince the garlic, dice the carrot, sweet potato, yam, and pumpkin or butternut squash.

Sauté Aromatics:
- In a large pot, heat vegetable oil over medium heat.
- Add chopped onions and minced garlic. Sauté until the onions are translucent.

Add Vegetables:
- Add diced carrots, sweet potato, yam, pumpkin or butternut squash, scallion, thyme, and bay leaves to the pot. Stir well.

Pour in Broth and Coconut Milk:
- Pour in vegetable or chicken broth and coconut milk. Stir to combine.

Simmer the Soup:
- Bring the soup to a boil, then reduce the heat to low. Let it simmer for about 15-20 minutes or until the vegetables are tender.

Add Callaloo and Okra:
- Add chopped callaloo (or substitute) and sliced okra to the pot. Stir well.
- If using Scotch bonnet pepper, you can add it whole to the pot for flavor. Remove it before serving if you don't want the soup too spicy.

Season and Serve:
- Season the soup with salt and black pepper to taste. Adjust the seasoning if necessary.
- Remove bay leaves and Scotch bonnet pepper if used whole.

Serve:
- Ladle the Callaloo Soup into bowls.
- Serve hot, accompanied by lime wedges for squeezing over the soup.

Enjoy this flavorful and nourishing Callaloo Soup, filled with a variety of vegetables and the richness of coconut milk. It's a comforting and hearty dish that brings the taste of the Caribbean to your table.

Breadfruit Salad: Roasted or boiled breadfruit tossed with herbs and spices.

Ingredients:

- 1 medium-sized breadfruit
- 2 tablespoons olive oil
- Salt and pepper to taste

For the Salad:

- 1 cup cherry tomatoes, halved
- 1 cucumber, diced
- 1 red onion, finely chopped
- 1 bell pepper (any color), diced
- 1/4 cup fresh cilantro, chopped
- 1/4 cup fresh parsley, chopped

For the Dressing:

- 3 tablespoons olive oil
- 2 tablespoons red wine vinegar
- 1 teaspoon Dijon mustard
- 1 clove garlic, minced
- Salt and pepper to taste

Instructions:

Roasting the Breadfruit:

    Preheat the Oven:
- Preheat your oven to 400°F (200°C).

    Prepare the Breadfruit:
- Peel the breadfruit and remove the core. Cut it into bite-sized cubes.

    Coat with Olive Oil:
- Place the breadfruit cubes on a baking sheet. Drizzle with olive oil, and season with salt and pepper. Toss to coat the breadfruit evenly.

    Roast the Breadfruit:
- Roast the breadfruit in the preheated oven for about 25-30 minutes or until golden brown and tender. Stir occasionally for even cooking.
- Remove from the oven and let it cool.

Assembling the Salad:

Prepare Vegetables:
- In a large bowl, combine the roasted breadfruit cubes with cherry tomatoes, cucumber, red onion, bell pepper, cilantro, and parsley.

Make the Dressing:
- In a small bowl, whisk together olive oil, red wine vinegar, Dijon mustard, minced garlic, salt, and pepper.

Toss the Salad:
- Pour the dressing over the salad ingredients and toss gently to coat everything evenly.

Serve:
- Transfer the Breadfruit Salad to a serving dish.
- Serve the salad at room temperature or chilled.

This Breadfruit Salad is a flavorful and refreshing dish that showcases the unique taste and texture of breadfruit. It makes a great side dish or a light meal on its own, perfect for warm weather or as a tropical-inspired addition to your menu.

Green Fig (Banana) Salad: Green bananas cooked and tossed in a spicy salad.

Ingredients:

- 4-5 green bananas (green figs)
- 1 tablespoon olive oil
- 1 small red onion, finely chopped
- 1 bell pepper (any color), finely chopped
- 1 small cucumber, diced
- 2 tomatoes, diced
- 2 tablespoons fresh cilantro or parsley, chopped
- 1 teaspoon ground cumin
- 1 teaspoon paprika
- 1/2 teaspoon cayenne pepper (adjust to taste)
- Salt and black pepper to taste
- Juice of 1 lime
- 2 tablespoons olive oil for dressing

Instructions:

Prepare the Green Bananas:
- Peel the green bananas and cut them into bite-sized pieces.

Cook the Bananas:
- In a pot of boiling water, add the green banana pieces. Cook for about 10-15 minutes or until they are fork-tender but still firm.
- Drain the cooked bananas and let them cool.

Prepare the Salad:
- In a large mixing bowl, combine the cooked green bananas, chopped red onion, bell pepper, cucumber, tomatoes, and fresh cilantro or parsley.

Make the Dressing:
- In a small bowl, whisk together olive oil, ground cumin, paprika, cayenne pepper, salt, black pepper, and lime juice.

Toss the Salad:
- Pour the dressing over the salad ingredients and toss gently to coat everything evenly.

Chill and Serve:
- Refrigerate the Green Fig Salad for at least 30 minutes before serving to allow the flavors to meld.

- Serve the salad chilled as a spicy and refreshing side dish.

This Green Fig Salad offers a unique twist by using green bananas, and the spicy dressing adds a flavorful kick. It's a great addition to your Caribbean-inspired menu or as a tasty side dish for any occasion.

Desserts and Sweets:

Rum Cake: Moist cake soaked in rum syrup.

Ingredients:

For the Cake:

- 1 cup unsalted butter, softened
- 2 cups granulated sugar
- 4 large eggs
- 3 cups all-purpose flour
- 1 teaspoon baking powder
- 1/2 teaspoon baking soda
- 1/2 teaspoon salt
- 1 cup buttermilk
- 1/2 cup dark rum
- 1 teaspoon vanilla extract

For the Rum Syrup:

- 1 cup granulated sugar
- 1/2 cup unsalted butter
- 1/4 cup water
- 1/2 cup dark rum

Instructions:

For the Cake:

Preheat the Oven:
- Preheat your oven to 325°F (160°C). Grease and flour a bundt cake pan.

Cream Butter and Sugar:
- In a large mixing bowl, cream together the softened butter and granulated sugar until light and fluffy.

Add Eggs:
- Add the eggs one at a time, beating well after each addition.

Combine Dry Ingredients:
- In a separate bowl, whisk together the flour, baking powder, baking soda, and salt.

Alternate Additions:
- Gradually add the dry ingredients to the butter-sugar mixture, alternating with buttermilk. Begin and end with the dry ingredients.
- Mix in the dark rum and vanilla extract until the batter is well combined.

Bake:
- Pour the batter into the prepared bundt pan and smooth the top.
- Bake in the preheated oven for approximately 60-70 minutes or until a toothpick inserted into the center comes out clean.

Cool:
- Allow the cake to cool in the pan for about 10 minutes, then transfer it to a wire rack to cool completely.

For the Rum Syrup:

Prepare Syrup:
- In a saucepan, combine sugar, butter, and water. Bring the mixture to a boil, stirring constantly.

Add Rum:
- Remove the saucepan from heat and stir in the dark rum.

Soak the Cake:
- While the cake is still warm, poke holes in it using a skewer or fork.
- Pour the warm rum syrup over the cake, allowing it to soak in. Continue until all the syrup is absorbed.

Serve:
- Let the cake cool and set before serving.

Enjoy this moist and flavorful Rum Cake, a delightful dessert with a rich and boozy kick!

Guava Duff: Guava-filled dumplings steamed or boiled.

Ingredients:

For the Dough:

- 3 cups all-purpose flour
- 1 tablespoon baking powder
- 1/2 teaspoon salt
- 1/2 cup unsalted butter, cold and diced
- 1/2 cup granulated sugar
- 1/2 cup milk
- 1 teaspoon vanilla extract

For the Guava Filling:

- 2 cups guava, mashed or pureed (strained if there are seeds)
- 1/2 cup granulated sugar
- 1/4 cup water
- 1 tablespoon lemon juice

For the Sauce:

- 1/2 cup unsalted butter
- 1/2 cup granulated sugar
- 1/2 cup water
- 1 teaspoon vanilla extract

Instructions:

For the Dough:

> Prepare the Dough:
> - In a large mixing bowl, whisk together the flour, baking powder, and salt.
> - Add the cold, diced butter to the flour mixture. Using a pastry cutter or your fingers, incorporate the butter until the mixture resembles coarse crumbs.

- Stir in the granulated sugar.
- Add the milk and vanilla extract, and mix until a soft dough forms.

Roll Out the Dough:
- On a floured surface, roll out the dough into a large rectangle, about 1/4-inch thick.

For the Guava Filling:

Make the Guava Filling:
- In a saucepan, combine the mashed or pureed guava, granulated sugar, water, and lemon juice.
- Cook over medium heat, stirring frequently, until the mixture thickens to a jam-like consistency. Remove from heat and let it cool.

Assemble the Guava Duff:
- Spread the guava filling evenly over the rolled-out dough.
- Roll the dough into a log, enclosing the guava filling. Seal the edges.
- Wrap the rolled dough in parchment paper or a clean kitchen towel, twisting the ends to secure it.

For Steaming or Boiling:

Steaming Method:
- Place the wrapped guava duff in a steamer and steam for about 1 to 1.5 hours, or until the dough is cooked through.

Boiling Method:
- Alternatively, you can boil the wrapped guava duff in a large pot of water for about 1.5 to 2 hours.

For the Sauce:

Prepare the Sauce:
- In a saucepan, combine butter, granulated sugar, water, and vanilla extract.
- Cook over medium heat, stirring until the sugar dissolves and the sauce thickens slightly.

Serve:
- Unwrap the guava duff and slice it into rounds.
- Pour the warm sauce over the slices before serving.

Enjoy this sweet and fruity Bahamian dessert, Guava Duff, with its soft and pillowy dough wrapped around a flavorful guava filling!

Tamarind Balls: Tamarind paste rolled into sweet and tangy balls.

Ingredients:

- 1 cup tamarind paste (seedless)
- 1/2 cup granulated sugar (adjust to taste)
- 1/4 teaspoon salt
- 1/2 teaspoon ground cumin (optional, for additional flavor)
- 1/4 cup water (for soaking tamarind paste)
- 1 cup fine granulated sugar (for coating)

Instructions:

Soak Tamarind Paste:
- If your tamarind paste is very thick, you can soak it in warm water to soften it. Place the tamarind paste in a bowl, add warm water, and let it soak for about 15-20 minutes. Stir occasionally to help break down the paste.

Strain Tamarind Paste:
- After soaking, strain the tamarind paste to remove any fibers or seeds. You should be left with a smooth tamarind concentrate.

Mix with Sugar and Salt:
- In a mixing bowl, combine the strained tamarind paste with granulated sugar and salt. Adjust the sugar according to your taste preferences.
- Optional: Add ground cumin for an extra layer of flavor.

Knead the Mixture:
- Knead the mixture well until it forms a smooth and pliable dough-like consistency. The sugar should be well incorporated.

Shape into Balls:
- Take small portions of the tamarind mixture and roll them into small balls between your palms. The size of the balls is based on your preference.

Coat with Sugar:
- Roll each tamarind ball in fine granulated sugar until well coated. This sugar coating adds sweetness and prevents the balls from sticking.

Let Them Set:
- Place the coated Tamarind Balls on a plate or tray, and let them set at room temperature for a few hours or in the refrigerator for quicker setting.

Serve:

- Once set, your Tamarind Balls are ready to be enjoyed as a sweet and tangy treat.

These Tamarind Balls are a delicious and unique snack with a perfect balance of sweetness and tanginess. They make a delightful addition to your selection of homemade candies and treats.

Sorrel Drink: Refreshing drink made from dried sorrel petals.

Ingredients:

- 2 cups dried sorrel petals
- 8 cups water
- 1 cup granulated sugar (adjust to taste)
- 1-2 cinnamon sticks
- 6-8 whole cloves
- 1-2 inches fresh ginger, peeled and sliced
- Orange peel or orange zest (optional, for added flavor)
- Rum or wine (optional, for a spiked version)

Instructions:

Rinse Sorrel Petals:
- Give the dried sorrel petals a quick rinse to remove any dust or debris.

Boil Water:
- In a large pot, bring the water to a boil.

Add Sorrel Petals:
- Once the water is boiling, add the dried sorrel petals to the pot.

Add Spices and Flavorings:
- Add cinnamon sticks, whole cloves, sliced ginger, and orange peel or orange zest (if using).
- Allow the mixture to simmer for about 15-20 minutes. The sorrel petals will release their vibrant red color and infuse the liquid with flavor.

Sweeten the Sorrel:
- After simmering, remove the pot from heat and sweeten the sorrel mixture with granulated sugar. Adjust the sugar to your desired level of sweetness.

Cool and Strain:
- Allow the sorrel mixture to cool to room temperature.
- Strain the liquid to remove the sorrel petals and spices, leaving you with a clear sorrel concentrate.

Chill:
- Refrigerate the sorrel concentrate until well chilled.

Serve:
- Serve the chilled sorrel concentrate over ice.
- Optional: Add rum or wine for an adult version of the drink.

Enjoy this festive and flavorful Sorrel Drink, perfect for quenching your thirst on warm days or serving at special occasions!

Gizzarda: Sweet coconut-filled pastries.

Ingredients:

For the Pastry Dough:

- 2 cups all-purpose flour
- 1/2 cup unsalted butter, cold and diced
- 1/2 cup granulated sugar
- 1/4 teaspoon salt
- 1 large egg yolk
- 1-2 tablespoons ice water (as needed)

For the Coconut Filling:

- 2 cups grated coconut (fresh or desiccated)
- 1 cup granulated sugar
- 1/2 teaspoon vanilla extract
- 1/4 teaspoon ground cinnamon
- 1/4 teaspoon ground nutmeg
- 1/4 cup water (if using desiccated coconut)

Instructions:

For the Pastry Dough:

Prepare the Dough:
- In a large bowl, combine the flour, diced cold butter, granulated sugar, and salt.
- Use your fingers or a pastry cutter to blend the ingredients until the mixture resembles breadcrumbs.

Add Egg Yolk:
- Add the egg yolk to the mixture and gently combine.

Form the Dough:
- Gradually add ice water, one tablespoon at a time, until the dough comes together. Be careful not to overwork the dough.

- Form the dough into a ball, wrap it in plastic wrap, and refrigerate for at least 30 minutes.

For the Coconut Filling:

Prepare the Coconut:
- If using fresh coconut, grate it finely. If using desiccated coconut, you can rehydrate it by mixing it with 1/4 cup of water and letting it sit for a few minutes.

Make the Filling:
- In a bowl, combine the grated coconut, granulated sugar, vanilla extract, ground cinnamon, and ground nutmeg. Mix well until the filling is uniform and slightly moist.

Assembling Gizzarda:

Preheat Oven:
- Preheat your oven to 350°F (175°C).

Roll Out Dough:
- On a floured surface, roll out the chilled dough to about 1/8 inch thickness.

Cut and Fill:
- Use a round cutter or a glass to cut out circles from the rolled-out dough.
- Place a small amount of the coconut filling in the center of each circle.

Fold and Seal:
- Fold the dough circle in half to form a half-moon shape. Press the edges to seal.

Shape and Bake:
- Use a fork to crimp the edges of the pastry.
- Place the filled pastries on a baking sheet and bake in the preheated oven for about 15-20 minutes or until golden brown.

Cool and Enjoy:
- Allow the Gizzarda to cool on a wire rack before serving.

These coconut-filled pastries are a delightful treat with a perfect balance of sweetness and tropical flavor. Enjoy your homemade Gizzarda!

Beverages:
Punch de Creme: A Trinidadian version of eggnog with rum.

Ingredients:

- 6 large eggs
- 1 cup granulated sugar (adjust to taste)
- 2 cups evaporated milk
- 1 cup condensed milk
- 1 cup white rum (adjust to taste)
- 1 teaspoon Angostura bitters (optional)
- 1 teaspoon grated nutmeg
- 1 teaspoon lime or lemon zest
- 1 teaspoon vanilla extract

Instructions:

Separate Egg Yolks:
- Separate the egg yolks from the egg whites. Place the egg yolks in a large mixing bowl.

Beat Eggs and Sugar:
- Using an electric mixer, beat the egg yolks until they become creamy and slightly thickened. Gradually add the granulated sugar and continue to beat until the mixture is pale and fluffy.

Add Condensed Milk:
- Gradually add the condensed milk to the egg and sugar mixture, continuing to beat until well combined.

Add Evaporated Milk:
- Slowly pour in the evaporated milk, continuing to beat the mixture.

Incorporate Rum and Flavorings:
- Add the white rum to the mixture. Adjust the quantity based on your preference for the strength of the drink.
- Add Angostura bitters (if using), grated nutmeg, lime or lemon zest, and vanilla extract. Mix well to combine.

Strain and Chill:
- Strain the Punch de Crème mixture through a fine-mesh sieve or cheesecloth to remove any lumps.

- Pour the strained mixture into bottles or a large jug and refrigerate for at least 2-3 hours, allowing the flavors to meld and the drink to chill.

Serve:
- Serve Punch de Crème chilled, over ice if desired.
- Garnish with a sprinkle of nutmeg on top.

Enjoy this Trinidadian Punch de Crème as a festive and flavorful addition to your holiday celebrations! The combination of eggs, milk, rum, and Caribbean spices creates a rich and indulgent drink that's perfect for toasting to special occasions.

Mauby: A traditional Caribbean beverage made from the bark of the mauby tree.

Ingredients:

- 1 cup dried mauby bark
- 8 cups water
- 1 cinnamon stick
- 4-6 cloves
- 1 star anise (optional)
- 1 cup granulated sugar (adjust to taste)
- 1 lime or lemon (for garnish)
- Ice cubes (optional)

Instructions:

Prepare the Mauby Bark:
- Rinse the dried mauby bark under cold water to remove any debris.

Boil the Mauby Bark:
- In a large pot, bring 8 cups of water to a boil.
- Add the dried mauby bark, cinnamon stick, cloves, and star anise (if using) to the boiling water.
- Reduce the heat to low and let the mixture simmer for about 45 minutes to 1 hour. The bark should release its flavor into the water.

Strain the Liquid:
- After simmering, remove the pot from heat and strain the liquid to separate the liquid from the mauby bark and spices. You should be left with a rich mauby concentrate.

Sweeten the Mauby:
- While the mauby concentrate is still warm, add granulated sugar to sweeten the drink. Adjust the amount of sugar to your taste preferences.
- Stir well to dissolve the sugar in the warm mauby concentrate.

Cool and Refrigerate:
- Allow the sweetened mauby concentrate to cool to room temperature.
- Once cooled, refrigerate the mauby concentrate for at least 2-3 hours, or until well chilled.

Serve:
- Pour the chilled mauby concentrate into glasses over ice cubes if desired.
- Garnish with a slice of lime or lemon.

Enjoy:

- Stir well before drinking, and enjoy the unique and refreshing flavor of Mauby!

Mauby is known for its distinct taste, which can be an acquired taste due to its bitterness. It's a popular choice during festive occasions or as a cooling drink on hot days in the Caribbean. Adjust the sweetness to your liking and savor this traditional beverage with its cultural significance.

Soursop Juice: Refreshing tropical fruit juice.

Ingredients:

- 2 cups soursop pulp (fresh or frozen)
- 4 cups water
- 1/2 cup granulated sugar (adjust to taste)
- 1 lime or lemon, juiced
- Ice cubes (optional)
- Mint leaves for garnish (optional)

Instructions:

Prepare the Soursop:
- If using fresh soursop, cut the fruit in half, remove the seeds, and scoop out the pulp. If using frozen soursop pulp, thaw it according to the package instructions.

Blend the Soursop:
- In a blender, combine the soursop pulp and water. Blend until the mixture is smooth.

Strain the Mixture:
- Strain the blended soursop mixture using a fine-mesh sieve or cheesecloth to remove any fibrous bits, leaving you with a smooth juice.

Sweeten the Juice:
- Pour the strained soursop juice back into the blender and add granulated sugar. Adjust the amount of sugar based on your sweetness preference.
- Blend again until the sugar is completely dissolved.

Add Citrus Juice:
- Squeeze the juice of a lime or lemon into the soursop mixture. This adds a bright citrus note to the juice.

Chill the Juice:
- Refrigerate the soursop juice for at least 1-2 hours to ensure it's well chilled.

Serve:
- Pour the chilled soursop juice into glasses over ice cubes if desired.
- Garnish with mint leaves for a fresh touch.

Enjoy:
- Stir well before drinking and enjoy the delicious and tropical flavor of Soursop Juice!

Soursop Juice is not only tasty but also packed with nutrients. It's a popular drink in many tropical regions and a fantastic way to enjoy the unique taste of soursop.

Pineapple Ginger Punch: Pineapple and ginger blended into a sweet and spicy drink.

Ingredients:

- 3 cups fresh pineapple chunks
- 2 tablespoons fresh ginger, peeled and grated
- 4 cups water
- 1/2 cup granulated sugar (adjust to taste)
- Juice of 2 limes or lemons
- Ice cubes
- Fresh mint leaves for garnish (optional)

Instructions:

Prepare Pineapple and Ginger:
- Peel and chop the fresh pineapple into chunks.
- Peel and grate the fresh ginger.

Blend Pineapple and Ginger:
- In a blender, combine the fresh pineapple chunks and grated ginger.
- Add water and blend until smooth.

Strain the Mixture:
- Strain the blended mixture using a fine-mesh sieve or cheesecloth to separate the liquid from any pulp.

Sweeten the Punch:
- Pour the strained pineapple and ginger liquid back into the blender.
- Add granulated sugar, adjusting the amount based on your sweetness preference.
- Blend again until the sugar is fully dissolved.

Add Citrus Juice:
- Squeeze the juice of limes or lemons into the blended mixture. This adds a zesty and citrusy flavor.

Chill the Punch:
- Refrigerate the Pineapple Ginger Punch for at least 1-2 hours to ensure it's well chilled.

Serve:
- Pour the chilled punch into glasses over ice cubes.
- Garnish with fresh mint leaves for a burst of freshness (optional).

Enjoy:

- Stir well before drinking and savor the sweet and spicy goodness of Pineapple Ginger Punch!

This refreshing beverage is perfect for hot days or as a unique addition to your party menu. The combination of pineapple and ginger creates a tropical and invigorating punch that's sure to be a hit.

Preserves and Pickles:

Mango Chutney: Spiced mango condiment.

Ingredients:

- 2 large ripe mangoes, peeled, pitted, and diced
- 1 cup granulated sugar
- 1/2 cup white vinegar
- 1 small onion, finely chopped
- 2 cloves garlic, minced
- 1 teaspoon ginger, grated
- 1/2 teaspoon mustard seeds
- 1/2 teaspoon cumin seeds
- 1/2 teaspoon ground turmeric
- 1/4 teaspoon red pepper flakes (adjust to taste)
- 1 cinnamon stick
- 3-4 whole cloves
- Salt to taste

Instructions:

Prepare Mangoes:
- Peel, pit, and dice the ripe mangoes.

Cook Mangoes:
- In a large saucepan, combine the diced mangoes, granulated sugar, white vinegar, chopped onion, minced garlic, grated ginger, mustard seeds, cumin seeds, ground turmeric, red pepper flakes, cinnamon stick, and whole cloves.

Simmer:
- Bring the mixture to a boil over medium-high heat, stirring to dissolve the sugar.
- Reduce the heat to low and let it simmer, uncovered, for about 45-60 minutes or until the chutney thickens. Stir occasionally.

Check Consistency:
- Test the consistency by placing a spoonful of the chutney on a cold plate. If it wrinkles and holds its shape, it's ready.

Adjust Seasoning:

- Taste the chutney and adjust the seasoning, adding salt or more red pepper flakes if needed.

Cool and Store:
- Remove the cinnamon stick and whole cloves. Let the chutney cool to room temperature.
- Once cooled, transfer the mango chutney to sterilized jars or airtight containers.

Refrigerate:
- Refrigerate the mango chutney for a few hours before using to allow the flavors to meld.

Serve:
- Serve Mango Chutney as a condiment with curries, grilled meats, sandwiches, or cheese.

This homemade Mango Chutney is bursting with flavor, combining the sweetness of mangoes with the warmth of spices. It's a versatile condiment that adds a delightful kick to your meals.

Pepper Sauce: Fiery hot sauce made with local peppers.

Ingredients:

- 1 cup hot peppers (such as Scotch bonnet, habanero, or your preferred spicy peppers), stemmed and chopped
- 2 cloves garlic, minced
- 1 small onion, chopped
- 1 cup white vinegar
- 1 teaspoon salt (adjust to taste)
- 1 teaspoon sugar (optional, to balance flavors)
- 1 tablespoon mustard seeds (optional, for added flavor)

Instructions:

Prepare Peppers:
- Wear gloves to handle hot peppers to avoid skin irritation. Stem and chop the hot peppers.

Blend Ingredients:
- In a blender, combine the chopped hot peppers, minced garlic, chopped onion, white vinegar, salt, sugar (if using), and mustard seeds (if using).

Blend until Smooth:
- Blend the ingredients until you achieve a smooth and uniform consistency.

Strain (Optional):
- If you prefer a smoother hot sauce, strain the mixture using a fine-mesh sieve or cheesecloth to remove any solids. This step is optional, and you can leave the sauce with some texture if desired.

Adjust Seasoning:
- Taste the hot sauce and adjust the salt and sugar according to your preference. Keep in mind that the flavors will intensify as the sauce sits.

Store in Bottles:
- Transfer the Pepper Sauce to sterilized bottles or jars with tight-fitting lids.

Let It Mature:
- Allow the Pepper Sauce to mature by storing it in a cool, dark place for at least a week. This allows the flavors to meld and intensify.

Shake Before Use:
- Shake the bottle before using the hot sauce to ensure an even distribution of flavors.

Enjoy:

- Use this Fiery Pepper Sauce sparingly to add heat to your favorite dishes. It pairs well with various cuisines, from Caribbean to Asian.

Note: Be cautious when handling hot peppers, especially if you have sensitive skin or eyes. Wash your hands thoroughly after handling them, and avoid touching your face.

Feel free to experiment with different types of hot peppers or additional ingredients like fruits or herbs to create a Pepper Sauce that suits your taste preferences!

Sorrel Jam: Sweet jam made from sorrel petals.

Ingredients:

- 4 cups sorrel petals (fresh or dried)
- 1 cup water
- 2 cups granulated sugar
- Juice of 1 lemon
- Zest of 1 lemon
- 1 teaspoon grated fresh ginger (optional)

Instructions:

Prepare Sorrel Petals:
- Rinse the sorrel petals under cold water to remove any debris.

Make Sorrel Infusion:
- In a saucepan, combine sorrel petals and water. Bring it to a boil.
- Reduce the heat to low and let it simmer for about 15-20 minutes to create a sorrel infusion. This allows the sorrel flavor to infuse into the water.

Strain the Sorrel Infusion:
- Strain the sorrel infusion using a fine-mesh sieve or cheesecloth to separate the liquid from the sorrel petals. You should be left with a vibrant sorrel liquid.

Prepare Sorrel Jam:
- In a clean saucepan, combine the sorrel infusion, granulated sugar, lemon juice, lemon zest, and grated fresh ginger (if using).
- Stir the mixture well to dissolve the sugar.

Cook the Jam:
- Bring the mixture to a boil over medium-high heat.
- Reduce the heat to low and let it simmer, stirring occasionally, until the jam thickens to your desired consistency. This may take around 30-40 minutes.

Check the Jam's Consistency:
- Test the jam's consistency by placing a small amount on a cold plate. If it wrinkles and holds its shape, it's ready.

Cool and Store:
- Allow the sorrel jam to cool to room temperature.
- Once cooled, transfer the jam to sterilized jars with tight-fitting lids.

Refrigerate:
- Refrigerate the sorrel jam for several hours or overnight to allow the flavors to meld.

Enjoy:
- Spread this unique Sorrel Jam on toast, scones, or use it as a sweet addition to desserts.

Sorrel Jam has a distinctive tangy flavor with floral and citrus notes, making it a delightful treat. Experiment with the recipe and adjust the sweetness or add other complementary flavors to make it your own!

Pickled Green Papaya: Tangy pickled green papaya.

Ingredients:

- 1 medium-sized green papaya, peeled, seeded, and julienned
- 1 cup white vinegar
- 1 cup water
- 1/2 cup granulated sugar
- 1 tablespoon salt
- 2 cloves garlic, minced
- 1 teaspoon grated ginger
- 1 teaspoon black peppercorns
- Red chili flakes or fresh red chili (optional, for heat)

Instructions:

Prepare Green Papaya:
- Peel the green papaya, cut it in half, and remove the seeds. Julienne the papaya into thin strips.

Make Pickling Liquid:
- In a saucepan, combine white vinegar, water, granulated sugar, salt, minced garlic, grated ginger, black peppercorns, and red chili flakes or fresh red chili if you want to add some heat.

Bring to a Boil:
- Bring the pickling liquid to a boil over medium-high heat, stirring to dissolve the sugar and salt.

Cool the Pickling Liquid:
- Allow the pickling liquid to cool to room temperature.

Combine with Green Papaya:
- Place the julienned green papaya in a clean, sterile glass jar or a non-reactive container.
- Pour the cooled pickling liquid over the green papaya, ensuring that the liquid covers the papaya completely.

Marinate:
- Let the green papaya marinate in the pickling liquid for at least 2-3 hours. For stronger flavor, you can refrigerate it for a day or two.

Store:
- Once marinated, store the Pickled Green Papaya in the refrigerator. It will last for a few weeks.

Serve:
- Serve the Pickled Green Papaya as a side dish, in salads, or as a topping for sandwiches and tacos.

This Pickled Green Papaya recipe provides a crisp and tangy condiment that can add a delightful contrast to a variety of dishes. Adjust the level of sweetness, salt, or spice to suit your taste preferences.

Street Food Classics:

Jamaican Beef Soup: Hearty soup with beef and vegetables.

Ingredients:

- 1 lb beef stew meat, cut into bite-sized pieces
- 2 tablespoons vegetable oil
- 1 onion, chopped
- 2 cloves garlic, minced
- 2 carrots, diced
- 2 potatoes, peeled and diced
- 1 cho-cho (chayote), peeled and diced
- 1 green plantain, peeled and sliced
- 2 ears of corn, cut into rounds
- 2 sprigs thyme
- 2 scallions, chopped
- 1 Scotch bonnet pepper, whole (optional, for heat)
- 1 cup cabbage, shredded
- 1 cup pumpkin or squash, diced
- 1 cup yam, peeled and diced
- 8 cups beef broth or water
- Salt and pepper to taste

Instructions:

Season and Brown the Beef:
- Season the beef stew meat with salt and pepper.
- In a large pot, heat vegetable oil over medium-high heat. Brown the beef on all sides. Remove and set aside.

Saute Aromatics:
- In the same pot, sauté chopped onion and minced garlic until softened.

Add Vegetables:
- Add carrots, potatoes, cho-cho, green plantain, corn rounds, thyme, scallions, Scotch bonnet pepper (if using), cabbage, pumpkin or squash, and yam to the pot.

Reintroduce Beef:
- Return the browned beef to the pot with the vegetables.

Pour in Broth:

- Pour beef broth or water into the pot, covering the ingredients.

Simmer:
- Bring the soup to a boil, then reduce the heat to low. Cover and let it simmer for about 1.5 to 2 hours, or until the beef and vegetables are tender.

Season and Adjust:
- Season the soup with salt and pepper to taste. Adjust the seasoning as needed.

Remove Scotch Bonnet (if using):
- If you used a whole Scotch bonnet pepper for heat, remove it from the soup before serving. Be cautious not to break the pepper, as it is very hot.

Serve:
- Ladle the Jamaican Beef Soup into bowls and serve hot.

This Jamaican Beef Soup is rich and comforting, filled with the flavors of Caribbean spices and a variety of vegetables. It's a perfect meal for a hearty and satisfying dinner. Adjust the spice level by controlling the use of Scotch bonnet pepper according to your taste preferences.

Trinidadian Corn Soup: Corn soup with dumplings and provision.

Ingredients:

- 1 cup dried split peas
- 1 lb chicken, diced (optional)
- 1 cup corn kernels (fresh or frozen)
- 1 large carrot, diced
- 1 large potato, peeled and diced
- 1 sweet potato, peeled and diced
- 1 dasheen (coco), peeled and diced
- 1 eddo (taro), peeled and diced
- 2 corn cobs, cut into rounds
- 1 onion, chopped
- 3 cloves garlic, minced
- 2 sprigs thyme
- 2 green onions, chopped
- 1 Scotch bonnet pepper, whole (optional, for heat)
- 2 dumplings (recipe below)
- Salt and pepper to taste
- 8-10 cups water or chicken broth

Dumplings:

- 1 cup all-purpose flour
- Water (as needed)
- Salt (a pinch)

Instructions:

Prepare Dumplings:
- In a bowl, combine the all-purpose flour, a pinch of salt, and add water gradually to form a soft dough.
- Knead the dough for a few minutes and shape it into small dumplings.
- Set the dumplings aside.

Cook Split Peas:
- Rinse the dried split peas and place them in a large pot with about 4 cups of water.

- Bring to a boil, then reduce the heat to simmer until the split peas are soft and partially broken down (about 30-40 minutes).

Add Chicken (if using):
- If using chicken, add diced chicken to the pot and cook until it's no longer pink.

Add Vegetables and Dumplings:
- Add corn kernels, diced carrot, potato, sweet potato, dasheen, eddo, corn rounds, onion, minced garlic, thyme, green onions, and the whole Scotch bonnet pepper (if using).
- Drop in the dumplings.

Pour in Water or Broth:
- Add enough water or chicken broth to cover all the ingredients in the pot. Adjust the liquid based on your desired soup consistency.

Simmer:
- Bring the soup to a boil, then reduce the heat to simmer. Cover and cook until all the vegetables are tender (about 30-40 minutes).

Season and Adjust:
- Season the soup with salt and pepper to taste. Adjust the seasoning as needed.

Remove Scotch Bonnet (if using):
- If a whole Scotch bonnet pepper was added for heat, remove it from the soup before serving.

Serve:
- Ladle the Trinidadian Corn Soup into bowls, ensuring each serving has a mix of vegetables, dumplings, and broth.

Enjoy this Trinidadian Corn Soup as a comforting and satisfying meal with a blend of flavors from the Caribbean!

Bahamian Conch Salad: Fresh conch salad with citrus and spices.

Ingredients:

- 1 lb fresh conch, cleaned and diced
- 1 cup red bell pepper, finely diced
- 1 cup green bell pepper, finely diced
- 1 cup tomato, finely diced
- 1 cup red onion, finely diced
- 1/2 cup cucumber, finely diced
- 1/2 cup celery, finely diced
- 1/2 cup fresh cilantro or parsley, chopped
- 1 Scotch bonnet pepper, finely chopped (adjust to taste)
- 1 cup fresh orange juice
- 1/2 cup fresh lime juice
- 1/4 cup fresh lemon juice
- Salt and pepper to taste
- 1 teaspoon ground cumin
- 1 teaspoon ground coriander
- 1 tablespoon olive oil
- Crackers or tortilla chips for serving

Instructions:

Prepare Conch:
- Ensure that the conch is cleaned thoroughly. Dice the conch into small, bite-sized pieces.

Mix Vegetables:
- In a large bowl, combine diced red bell pepper, green bell pepper, tomato, red onion, cucumber, celery, and fresh cilantro or parsley.

Add Conch:
- Add the diced conch to the vegetable mixture.

Prepare Citrus Dressing:
- In a separate bowl, whisk together fresh orange juice, lime juice, and lemon juice.

Season and Spice:
- Add chopped Scotch bonnet pepper, ground cumin, ground coriander, salt, and pepper to the citrus dressing. Adjust the spice level to your taste.

Combine Ingredients:
- Pour the citrus dressing over the conch and vegetable mixture.
- Drizzle olive oil over the salad.

Toss and Marinate:
- Gently toss the ingredients to coat them evenly with the citrus dressing.
- Allow the conch salad to marinate in the refrigerator for at least 30 minutes to let the flavors meld.

Serve:
- Just before serving, give the Bahamian Conch Salad a final toss.
- Serve the conch salad in individual bowls or on a platter.

Enjoy:
- Serve with crackers or tortilla chips on the side and enjoy the fresh and zesty flavors of Bahamian Conch Salad!

Bahamian Conch Salad is a popular dish in the Bahamas and throughout the Caribbean, known for its vibrant colors and bold flavors. It's a perfect appetizer or light meal, especially on a warm day. Adjust the ingredients and spice level according to your preferences.

Bake and Shark: Fried shark sandwich with various toppings.

Ingredients:

For the Fried Shark:

- 1 lb shark fillets, cut into manageable pieces
- 2 cups all-purpose flour
- 1 teaspoon baking powder
- 1 teaspoon ground turmeric
- Salt and pepper to taste
- Vegetable oil for frying

For the Bake (Fried Bread):

- 2 cups all-purpose flour
- 1 tablespoon baking powder
- 1/2 teaspoon salt
- Water (enough to make a soft dough)
- Vegetable oil for frying

For Toppings:

- Shredded lettuce
- Sliced tomatoes
- Sliced cucumbers
- Shredded cabbage
- Chopped cilantro or parsley
- Pineapple slices
- Tamarind sauce or your favorite hot sauce
- Garlic sauce (optional)

Instructions:

For the Fried Shark:

In a bowl, mix flour, baking powder, ground turmeric, salt, and pepper.
Coat shark pieces in the flour mixture, ensuring they are evenly covered.
In a deep pan, heat vegetable oil for frying over medium heat.

Fry the shark pieces until golden brown and cooked through. This usually takes about 3-5 minutes per side.
Remove fried shark from the oil and place on paper towels to absorb excess oil.

For the Bake (Fried Bread):

In a bowl, mix flour, baking powder, and salt.
Gradually add water, stirring continuously, until a soft dough forms.
Knead the dough on a floured surface until smooth.
Divide the dough into small balls and flatten them into rounds.
Heat vegetable oil in a pan over medium heat and fry the bread rounds until they puff up and turn golden brown.
Remove the fried bread and place them on paper towels to drain excess oil.

Assembling the Bake and Shark:

Take a piece of fried bread (bake) and cut it open, creating a pocket.
Insert a piece of fried shark into the pocket.
Add your desired toppings such as shredded lettuce, sliced tomatoes, sliced cucumbers, shredded cabbage, chopped cilantro or parsley, pineapple slices, tamarind sauce, and garlic sauce.
Optionally, add your favorite hot sauce for extra heat.
Close the sandwich and serve immediately.

Enjoy your homemade Bake and Shark with a delightful combination of crispy fried shark, flavorful toppings, and delicious sauces!

Breakfast and Brunch:

Doubles: Fried bread with curried chickpeas.

Ingredients:

For the Fried Bread (Bara):

- 2 cups all-purpose flour
- 1 teaspoon baking powder
- 1/2 teaspoon ground turmeric
- 1 teaspoon curry powder
- 1/2 teaspoon salt
- Water (enough to make a soft dough)
- Vegetable oil for frying

For the Curried Chickpeas (Channa):

- 2 cans (15 oz each) chickpeas, drained and rinsed
- 1 onion, finely chopped
- 2 cloves garlic, minced
- 1 tablespoon curry powder
- 1 teaspoon ground cumin
- 1 teaspoon ground coriander
- 1 teaspoon ground turmeric
- 1/2 teaspoon cayenne pepper (adjust to taste)
- 1 cup water
- Salt and pepper to taste
- Vegetable oil for cooking

For Toppings:

- Shredded lettuce
- Chopped cilantro or parsley
- Tamarind sauce or your favorite hot sauce

Instructions:

For the Fried Bread (Bara):

- In a large bowl, combine flour, baking powder, ground turmeric, curry powder, and salt.
- Gradually add water, stirring continuously, until a soft dough forms.
- Knead the dough on a floured surface until smooth.
- Divide the dough into small balls and flatten them into rounds.
- Heat vegetable oil in a pan over medium heat and fry the bread rounds until they puff up and turn golden brown.
- Remove the fried bread and place them on paper towels to drain excess oil.

For the Curried Chickpeas (Channa):

- In a pan, heat vegetable oil over medium heat.
- Add chopped onions and minced garlic, sauté until softened.
- Stir in curry powder, ground cumin, ground coriander, ground turmeric, and cayenne pepper.
- Add drained chickpeas to the pan and toss to coat them in the spice mixture.
- Pour in water, bring to a simmer, and let it cook for about 15-20 minutes or until the chickpeas are tender.
- Season with salt and pepper to taste.

Assembling the Doubles:

- Take a piece of fried bread (bara) and place a spoonful of curried chickpeas (channa) in the center.
- Add shredded lettuce, chopped cilantro or parsley, and drizzle with tamarind sauce or hot sauce.
- Optionally, fold another piece of fried bread over the top to create a sandwich.
- Serve immediately and enjoy!

Doubles are not only delicious but also customizable with various toppings and sauces.

Enjoy this Trinidadian street food classic at home!

Jamaican Bammy: Cassava flatbread served with fish or ackee.

Ingredients:

- 2 cups cassava flour
- 1/2 teaspoon salt
- 1 cup coconut milk
- Vegetable oil (for greasing)

Instructions:

Prepare Cassava Dough:
- In a mixing bowl, combine cassava flour and salt.

Add Coconut Milk:
- Gradually add coconut milk to the cassava flour mixture, stirring continuously to avoid lumps.

Knead the Dough:
- Knead the mixture into a smooth, pliable dough.

Shape into Discs:
- Divide the dough into small balls and shape them into discs, about 4-6 inches in diameter.

Cooking Bammy:
- Heat a griddle or a flat pan over medium heat.
- Grease the hot surface with a bit of vegetable oil.
- Place the shaped bammy discs on the griddle and cook for about 5-7 minutes on each side or until golden brown.
- Optionally, you can finish cooking the bammy in the oven. Preheat the oven to 350°F (175°C) and bake for an additional 10-15 minutes until fully cooked.

Serve:
- Once cooked, serve the bammy hot with your choice of accompaniment, such as fish or ackee and saltfish.

To Serve with Fish:

Grill or Fry Fish:
- Grill or fry your choice of fish until cooked through. Popular choices include snapper or parrotfish.

Serve with Bammy:

- Serve the grilled or fried fish over the hot bammy.

Garnish:
- Garnish with fresh lime or lemon wedges.

To Serve with Ackee and Saltfish:

Prepare Ackee and Saltfish:
- Prepare the traditional Jamaican dish of ackee and saltfish. Sauté ackee with flaked saltfish, onions, tomatoes, and seasonings.

Serve with Bammy:
- Serve the hot bammy alongside the ackee and saltfish.

Enjoy:
- Enjoy this classic Jamaican dish with the unique texture and flavor of bammy!

Bammy adds a wonderful starchy element to your meal, and its subtle cassava flavor complements the savory dishes it's often served with.

Belizean Johnny Cakes: Fried dough served with various accompaniments.

Ingredients:

- 2 cups all-purpose flour
- 1 tablespoon baking powder
- 1/2 teaspoon salt
- 2 tablespoons sugar
- 2 tablespoons shortening or butter, cold
- 3/4 cup milk (adjust as needed)
- Vegetable oil for frying

Instructions:

Prepare the Dough:
- In a large mixing bowl, combine the all-purpose flour, baking powder, salt, and sugar.

Incorporate Shortening:
- Add the cold shortening or butter to the dry ingredients. Use your fingers or a pastry cutter to cut the shortening into the flour until the mixture resembles coarse crumbs.

Add Milk:
- Gradually add the milk to the flour mixture, stirring with a fork until a soft dough forms. Add more milk if needed to bring the dough together.

Knead the Dough:
- Turn the dough out onto a floured surface and knead it lightly until it comes together.

Shape into Rounds:
- Pinch off pieces of dough and shape them into rounds, about 3 inches in diameter and 1/2 inch thick. You can make them smaller or larger based on your preference.

Heat Oil:
- In a frying pan, heat vegetable oil over medium heat. The oil should be hot but not smoking.

Fry Johnny Cakes:
- Carefully place the shaped dough rounds into the hot oil. Fry each side until golden brown, which takes about 2-3 minutes per side.

Drain and Serve:

- Remove the Johnny Cakes from the oil and place them on paper towels to drain any excess oil.

Serve Warm:
- Serve the Belizean Johnny Cakes warm. They are delicious on their own or can be served with various accompaniments.

Accompaniments:

- Cheese: Belizean Johnny Cakes are often served with cheese, either on the side or as a sandwich.
- Jam or Jelly: Spread your favorite jam or jelly on top for a sweet variation.
- Butter or Honey: Serve with a generous pat of butter or a drizzle of honey for a simple and tasty option.
- Dinner Accompaniment: They can also be served alongside savory dishes, stews, or soups.

Belizean Johnny Cakes are versatile and can be enjoyed in various ways – sweet or savory. They make a wonderful addition to breakfast or as a side dish for other meals.

Grilled Delicacies:

Jamaican Escovitch Fish: Fried fish topped with spicy pickled vegetables.

Ingredients:

For Fried Fish:

- 2 lbs whole fish (snapper or grunt), scaled, cleaned, and scored
- Salt and pepper to taste
- 1 cup all-purpose flour, for coating
- Vegetable oil for frying

For Escovitch Sauce:

- 1 large carrot, julienned
- 1 large onion, thinly sliced
- 1 bell pepper (red or yellow), thinly sliced
- 1 Scotch bonnet pepper, thinly sliced (seeds removed for less heat)
- 1 cup white vinegar
- 1/2 cup water
- 2 teaspoons sugar
- 1 teaspoon salt
- 1 teaspoon whole allspice
- 4 pimento seeds
- 4 sprigs thyme
- Vegetable oil for sautéing

Instructions:

For Fried Fish:

    Clean and Score Fish:
- Clean the fish, remove scales, gut, and score the fish on both sides.

    Season and Coat:
- Season the fish with salt and pepper. Coat each fish with flour, shaking off any excess.

    Fry Fish:

- In a large skillet or deep fryer, heat vegetable oil over medium-high heat. Fry the fish until golden brown and cooked through, about 5-7 minutes per side depending on the size of the fish. Drain on paper towels.

For Escovitch Sauce:

Prepare Vegetables:
- In a pan, heat a few tablespoons of vegetable oil over medium heat. Add julienned carrots, sliced onions, sliced bell pepper, and sliced Scotch bonnet pepper. Sauté until the vegetables are slightly softened but still vibrant.

Make Pickling Liquid:
- In a separate saucepan, combine white vinegar, water, sugar, salt, allspice, pimento seeds, and thyme. Bring to a boil and then simmer for a couple of minutes.

Combine and Cool:
- Pour the pickling liquid over the sautéed vegetables. Allow the mixture to cool.

Assemble Escovitch Sauce:
- Once the pickled vegetables have cooled, spoon them over the fried fish.

Marinate:
- Allow the fish to marinate in the escovitch sauce for at least 30 minutes. This allows the flavors to meld.

Serve:
- Serve the Jamaican Escovitch Fish with your favorite side dishes. It's often enjoyed with bread, bammy, or fried plantains.

Tips:

- Be cautious when handling Scotch bonnet peppers, as they are very hot. Wear gloves and wash hands thoroughly after handling.
- Adjust the amount of Scotch bonnet pepper to control the level of spiciness in the dish.

Jamaican Escovitch Fish is a delightful combination of crispy fried fish and tangy, spicy pickled vegetables, creating a burst of flavors with each bite. Enjoy this traditional Jamaican dish for a satisfying and flavorful meal!

Bajan Fish Cutter: Fried fish sandwich with Bajan hot sauce.

Ingredients:

For Fried Fish:

- 2 lbs firm white fish fillets (snapper, kingfish, or similar)
- 1 cup all-purpose flour
- 1 teaspoon Bajan seasoning (or a mix of garlic powder, onion powder, thyme, paprika, salt, and pepper)
- Vegetable oil for frying

For Bajan Hot Sauce:

- 4-6 Scotch bonnet peppers, seeds removed and finely chopped
- 1 small onion, finely chopped
- 2 cloves garlic, minced
- 1 cup white vinegar
- 1 tablespoon yellow mustard
- 1 tablespoon brown sugar
- Salt and pepper to taste

For Assembling:

- Fresh Bajan salt bread or your preferred bread rolls
- Lettuce leaves
- Tomato slices
- Pickles or cucumbers (optional)

Instructions:

For Fried Fish:

Clean and Season Fish:
- Clean and pat dry the fish fillets. Season them with Bajan seasoning (or your homemade spice mix).

Coat with Flour:

- In a shallow dish, coat each fish fillet with all-purpose flour, shaking off excess.

Fry Fish:
- In a pan or deep fryer, heat vegetable oil over medium-high heat. Fry the fish until golden brown and cooked through, approximately 3-4 minutes per side. Drain on paper towels.

For Bajan Hot Sauce:

Prepare Hot Sauce:
- In a small saucepan, combine finely chopped Scotch bonnet peppers, chopped onion, minced garlic, white vinegar, yellow mustard, brown sugar, salt, and pepper.

Simmer:
- Bring the mixture to a simmer over medium heat, stirring occasionally. Let it simmer for about 10-15 minutes until the sauce thickens slightly.

Cool:
- Allow the Bajan hot sauce to cool completely. Adjust salt and pepper to taste.

For Assembling:

Prepare Bread Rolls:
- If you can find Bajan salt bread, split it in half horizontally. If not, use your preferred bread rolls.

Assemble Sandwich:
- On the bottom half of the bread, place a lettuce leaf, followed by a fried fish fillet.
- Add tomato slices and pickles or cucumbers if desired.
- Spoon a generous amount of Bajan hot sauce over the fish.

Top and Serve:
- Place the top half of the bread over the fillings to complete the sandwich.
- Serve the Bajan Fish Cutter immediately, and enjoy the bold flavors!

Note:

- Adjust the amount of Scotch bonnet pepper in the hot sauce to control the level of spiciness according to your preference.

A Bajan Fish Cutter is a delightful combination of crispy fried fish, vibrant Bajan hot sauce, and fresh vegetables, all nestled in a soft bread roll. It's a quintessential Bajan street food experience that you can recreate at home.

Antiguan Pepperpot: Spiced pork stew.

Ingredients:

- 2 lbs pork, cut into bite-sized pieces
- 1 cup okra, sliced
- 1 cup callaloo or spinach, chopped
- 1 cup eggplant, diced
- 1 cup pumpkin or butternut squash, diced
- 1 cup dasheen or taro root, diced
- 1 cup yams, diced
- 1 cup sweet potatoes, diced
- 1 cup cassava, diced
- 1 cup eddoes, diced
- 1 onion, chopped
- 4 cloves garlic, minced
- 2 sprigs thyme
- 2 bay leaves
- 1 Scotch bonnet pepper, whole (for flavor, remove before serving for milder heat)
- 1 cup coconut milk
- 4 cups beef or vegetable broth
- Salt and pepper to taste
- 2 tablespoons oil for cooking

Instructions:

Prepare the Pork:
- Season the pork pieces with salt and pepper.

Sear the Pork:
- In a large pot, heat the oil over medium-high heat. Brown the pork pieces on all sides until they develop a golden crust. Remove the pork from the pot and set it aside.

Sauté Aromatics:
- In the same pot, add chopped onions and minced garlic. Sauté until the onions are translucent.

Add Vegetables:

- Add the okra, callaloo or spinach, eggplant, pumpkin or butternut squash, dasheen or taro root, yams, sweet potatoes, cassava, and eddoes to the pot. Stir well to combine.

Return Pork to Pot:
- Return the seared pork pieces to the pot.

Season:
- Add thyme, bay leaves, whole Scotch bonnet pepper, and coconut milk. Pour in the beef or vegetable broth.

Simmer:
- Bring the mixture to a boil, then reduce the heat to low. Cover the pot and let it simmer for about 1.5 to 2 hours, or until the pork is tender and the flavors have melded together.

Adjust Seasoning:
- Adjust the seasoning with salt and pepper to taste. You can also remove the Scotch bonnet pepper if you want to reduce the spiciness.

Serve:
- Serve the Antiguan Pepperpot hot over rice or with bread.

Note:

- The traditional method involves using a "pepperpot plant," but if unavailable, you can use a whole Scotch bonnet pepper for flavor and remove it before serving for milder heat.
- Feel free to customize the choice of vegetables based on availability and personal preference.

Antiguan Pepperpot is a hearty and comforting stew, perfect for warming up on a chilly day. The blend of spices and the variety of vegetables make it a flavorful and wholesome dish.

Celebration Dishes:

Bajan Black Cake: Dark fruitcake soaked in rum.

Ingredients:

For Fruit Soaking:

- 2 cups mixed dried fruits (raisins, currants, prunes, dates, cherries)
- 1 cup rum (dark rum or a mixture of dark and light rum)
- 1 cup red wine
- 1 cup port wine

For Cake Batter:

- 1 cup unsalted butter, softened
- 1 cup brown sugar
- 6 large eggs
- 2 cups all-purpose flour
- 1 teaspoon baking powder
- 1 teaspoon ground nutmeg
- 1 teaspoon ground cinnamon
- 1/2 teaspoon allspice
- 1/2 cup breadcrumbs
- 1/2 cup molasses
- 1/4 cup browning (a Caribbean-style caramel sauce)
- 1 cup finely grated coconut (optional)
- 1 cup mixed nuts (walnuts, almonds), chopped

For Rum Soaking (after baking):

- 1 cup rum (for soaking)

Instructions:

1. Preparing the Fruit:

- Combine the mixed dried fruits with rum, red wine, and port wine in a large bowl. Let it soak for at least a few days to allow the fruits to absorb the flavors.

2. Making the Cake Batter:

   Preheat the oven to 325°F (163°C). Grease and line a cake pan with parchment paper.
   In a large mixing bowl, cream together the softened butter and brown sugar until light and fluffy.
   Add the eggs one at a time, beating well after each addition.
   In a separate bowl, whisk together the flour, baking powder, nutmeg, cinnamon, and allspice.
   Gradually add the dry ingredients to the butter and sugar mixture, mixing well.
   Fold in the breadcrumbs, molasses, browning, grated coconut (if using), and the soaked fruit mixture (including the liquid).
   Stir in the chopped nuts.

3. Baking the Cake:

   Pour the batter into the prepared cake pan and smooth the top.
   Bake in the preheated oven for 2 to 2.5 hours or until a toothpick inserted into the center comes out clean.
   Allow the cake to cool completely in the pan.

4. Soaking the Cake in Rum:

   Once the cake is cooled, use a skewer or fork to poke holes all over the surface.
   Slowly pour 1 cup of rum over the cake, allowing it to seep into the holes.
   Let the cake soak in the rum for at least a day or longer for a richer flavor.

5. Serving:

   - Slice and serve the Bajan Black Cake on special occasions or celebrations.

Note:

   - The longer the cake is allowed to soak in rum, the more intense the flavor will be. Some people even soak the fruit mixture for months before baking the cake.
   - Bajan Black Cake is often made well in advance of special occasions to allow time for soaking and maturing, enhancing the flavor.

Guyanese Pepperpot: Spicy meat stew traditionally served at Christmas.

Ingredients:

- 3 lbs beef, cut into bite-sized pieces
- 1 lb pork, cut into bite-sized pieces
- 1 cow heel (optional), cut into pieces
- 1 cup cassareep (a thick, black liquid made from cassava)
- 1 large onion, chopped
- 4 cloves garlic, minced
- 1-2 Scotch bonnet peppers, whole (adjust based on spice preference)
- 1 cinnamon stick
- 4 cloves
- 4 sprigs thyme
- 2 bay leaves
- Salt and pepper to taste
- Water for boiling

Instructions:

Prepare the Meat:
- Clean and wash the beef, pork, and cow heel (if using). Cut them into bite-sized pieces.

Boil the Meat:
- In a large pot, place the beef, pork, and cow heel. Cover with water and bring to a boil. Allow it to boil for about 10 minutes.

Discard the First Boil:
- Drain the meat and discard the water. This helps remove excess fat and impurities.

Second Boil:
- Fill the pot with fresh water, covering the meat again. Add the chopped onion, minced garlic, Scotch bonnet peppers, cinnamon stick, cloves, thyme, bay leaves, salt, and pepper.

Simmer:
- Bring the pot to a simmer and let it cook for about 2-3 hours or until the meat is tender. Skim off any foam that rises to the surface.

Add Cassareep:

- Pour in the cassareep and stir well. Continue to simmer for an additional 30 minutes to allow the flavors to meld.

Check and Adjust:
- Taste the Pepperpot and adjust the seasoning if necessary. If you prefer a thicker consistency, you can let it simmer for a bit longer.

Serve:
- Guyanese Pepperpot is traditionally served with cassava bread. Enjoy it during Christmas celebrations or any special occasion.

Note:

- Cassareep is a key ingredient in Pepperpot and gives it its distinct flavor. If you can't find cassareep, you can try making a substitute by boiling cassava juice until it thickens and darkens.
- Adjust the number of Scotch bonnet peppers based on your spice tolerance. You can also remove the seeds for less heat.

Jamaican Sorrel Chicken: Chicken cooked in a sorrel-infused sauce.

Ingredients:

- 2 lbs chicken pieces (drumsticks, thighs, or a mix)
- 2 cups sorrel petals (fresh or dried)
- 1 large onion, finely chopped
- 3 cloves garlic, minced
- 1 Scotch bonnet pepper, finely chopped (adjust to taste)
- 1 cup chicken broth
- 1/2 cup coconut milk
- 2 tablespoons vegetable oil
- 2 teaspoons fresh thyme leaves
- 1 teaspoon grated fresh ginger
- Salt and pepper to taste
- Lime wedges for serving

Instructions:

Prepare Sorrel Petals:
- If using fresh sorrel, remove the petals from the calyx. If using dried sorrel, rinse them under cold water.

Marinate Chicken:
- Season the chicken pieces with salt and pepper. Set them aside to marinate for at least 30 minutes.

Sauté Aromatics:
- In a large pot or Dutch oven, heat the vegetable oil over medium heat. Add chopped onions and sauté until they become translucent.

Add Garlic, Ginger, and Scotch Bonnet:
- Stir in minced garlic, grated ginger, and chopped Scotch bonnet pepper. Sauté for another 2-3 minutes until fragrant.

Brown Chicken:
- Add the marinated chicken pieces to the pot. Brown them on all sides to develop a golden color.

Infuse Sorrel Flavor:
- Add the sorrel petals to the pot. Stir well to infuse the sorrel flavor into the chicken.

Pour in Liquid:

- Pour in chicken broth and coconut milk. Stir to combine.

Simmer:
- Bring the mixture to a simmer. Cover the pot and let it simmer over low to medium heat for about 30-40 minutes or until the chicken is fully cooked and tender.

Adjust Seasoning:
- Taste the sauce and adjust the seasoning with salt and pepper as needed.

Finish with Thyme:
- Stir in fresh thyme leaves for a burst of flavor.

Serve:
- Serve the Jamaican Sorrel Chicken over rice or with your favorite side dishes. Garnish with additional thyme leaves and lime wedges.

Enjoy:
- Enjoy this flavorful and uniquely Jamaican dish with the tangy essence of sorrel!

Jamaican Sorrel Chicken is a festive and flavorful dish that brings a taste of the Caribbean to your table. The combination of spices, herbs, and sorrel creates a vibrant and delicious culinary experience.

Local Flavors:

Green Seasoning: Blend of fresh herbs and spices used as a marinade.

Ingredients:

- 1 bunch fresh cilantro (coriander), roughly chopped
- 1 bunch fresh parsley, roughly chopped
- 4-6 scallions (green onions), chopped
- 1 small onion, chopped
- 4 cloves garlic, peeled
- 1-2 Scotch bonnet peppers (adjust based on spice preference)
- 1 tablespoon fresh thyme leaves
- 1 tablespoon fresh oregano leaves (optional)
- 1 teaspoon ground allspice
- 1 teaspoon ground black pepper
- 1 teaspoon salt (adjust to taste)
- 1/2 cup olive oil or vegetable oil
- Juice of 1-2 limes or lemons

Instructions:

Prepare Herbs:
- Wash and roughly chop the cilantro and parsley.

Blend Ingredients:
- In a blender or food processor, combine cilantro, parsley, scallions, onion, garlic, Scotch bonnet peppers, thyme, oregano (if using), allspice, black pepper, and salt.

Blend to Smooth Consistency:
- Pulse or blend the ingredients until you achieve a smooth, vibrant green paste.

Adjust Thickness:
- If the mixture is too thick, you can add a bit of water to achieve the desired consistency.

Add Oil and Citrus:
- While the blender is running, gradually pour in the olive oil or vegetable oil. Then, add the juice of the limes or lemons.

Blend Until Combined:

- Continue blending until the oil and citrus are well incorporated, and you have a smooth and well-mixed green seasoning.

Taste and Adjust:
- Taste the green seasoning and adjust the salt, pepper, or citrus juice according to your preference.

Store:
- Transfer the green seasoning to a clean, airtight container. It can be stored in the refrigerator for up to a week or frozen in smaller portions for longer storage.

Usage:

- Green seasoning can be used as a marinade for meats, fish, or vegetables before grilling, roasting, or pan-frying.
- It can also be used as a base for soups, stews, or sauces to add depth of flavor.
- Some people even use it as a condiment or dipping sauce for various dishes.

Green seasoning is a versatile and aromatic addition to Caribbean and Latin American cuisines, adding a burst of fresh flavors to a wide range of dishes. Adjust the spice level and herb proportions to suit your taste preferences.

Belizean Rice and Beans: Classic rice and beans dish cooked in coconut milk.

Ingredients:

- 2 cups long-grain rice
- 1 cup red kidney beans, soaked overnight or canned
- 1 cup coconut milk
- 1 onion, finely chopped
- 2 cloves garlic, minced
- 1 bell pepper, finely chopped
- 1-2 sprigs fresh thyme (or 1 teaspoon dried thyme)
- 2 bay leaves
- 1 teaspoon ground cumin
- 1 teaspoon paprika
- 1 teaspoon ground black pepper
- Salt to taste
- 2 tablespoons vegetable oil
- 2 cups water (or vegetable or chicken broth for added flavor)

Instructions:

Prepare Beans:
- If using dried beans, soak them overnight in water. Rinse and drain before cooking. If using canned beans, rinse them under cold water.

Sauté Aromatics:
- In a large pot or Dutch oven, heat vegetable oil over medium heat. Add chopped onions, minced garlic, and bell pepper. Sauté until the vegetables are softened.

Add Rice and Spices:
- Add the rice to the pot and stir to coat it with the sautéed vegetables. Allow the rice to toast slightly for about 2-3 minutes.

Incorporate Spices:
- Stir in ground cumin, paprika, black pepper, thyme, and bay leaves. Mix well to distribute the spices evenly.

Add Coconut Milk and Water:
- Pour in the coconut milk and water (or broth). Stir the mixture thoroughly.

Add Beans:

- Add the soaked or canned beans to the pot. Stir to combine all the ingredients.

Bring to a Boil:
- Increase the heat to high and bring the mixture to a boil.

Reduce Heat and Simmer:
- Once boiling, reduce the heat to low, cover the pot with a tight-fitting lid, and let it simmer for about 20-25 minutes or until the rice is cooked and the liquid is absorbed.

Fluff and Rest:
- Once cooked, fluff the rice with a fork, cover the pot, and let it rest for 5-10 minutes to allow the flavors to meld.

Serve:
- Serve Belizean Rice and Beans as a delicious side dish or as a main course with your favorite protein.

Belizean Rice and Beans is a comforting and flavorful dish that reflects the vibrant culinary culture of Belize. The combination of coconut milk and aromatic spices adds a unique richness to this classic dish. Enjoy it on its own or as a side dish to complement a variety of meals.

Curry Crab and Dumplings: Crab cooked in a flavorful curry sauce.

Ingredients:

For Curry Crab:

- 2 lbs crab, cleaned and cracked
- 2 tablespoons curry powder
- 1 large onion, finely chopped
- 3 cloves garlic, minced
- 1 thumb-sized piece of ginger, grated
- 1 Scotch bonnet pepper, finely chopped (adjust to taste)
- 1 tablespoon tomato paste
- 1 can (14 oz) coconut milk
- 1 cup vegetable or seafood broth
- 2 tablespoons vegetable oil
- 1 tablespoon all-purpose seasoning (optional)
- Salt and pepper to taste
- Fresh cilantro or parsley for garnish

For Dumplings:

- 2 cups all-purpose flour
- 1 teaspoon baking powder
- 1/2 teaspoon salt
- Water, as needed (approximately 1 cup)

Instructions:

For Dumplings:

In a bowl, combine the all-purpose flour, baking powder, and salt.
Gradually add water and knead the mixture until a soft dough forms. Adjust the water or flour if needed.
Divide the dough into small portions and shape them into dumplings.
In a pot of boiling water, drop the dumplings and cook until they float to the surface. Remove them with a slotted spoon and set aside.

For Curry Crab:

Clean and crack the crab, removing the shells as much as possible.
In a large pot or Dutch oven, heat vegetable oil over medium heat.
Add chopped onions and sauté until they become translucent.
Stir in minced garlic, grated ginger, and chopped Scotch bonnet pepper. Sauté for another 2-3 minutes until fragrant.
Add curry powder and tomato paste. Mix well to form a thick curry paste.
Add the cleaned crab to the pot, stirring to coat the crab with the curry paste.
Pour in coconut milk and vegetable or seafood broth. Season with all-purpose seasoning (if using), salt, and pepper.
Bring the mixture to a simmer and let it cook for about 20-25 minutes or until the crab is cooked through and the flavors have melded.
Adjust seasoning to taste and sprinkle fresh cilantro or parsley for garnish.

Serve:

Serve the Curry Crab over a bed of rice or with the prepared dumplings. Enjoy this delicious and savory dish that highlights the flavors of crab and the aromatic curry sauce.

St. Lucian Bread Pudding: Sweet bread pudding with local spices.

Ingredients:

- 6 cups bread cubes (stale or day-old bread)
- 2 cups milk
- 1 cup coconut milk
- 3/4 cup brown sugar
- 3 eggs, beaten
- 1 teaspoon vanilla extract
- 1/2 teaspoon ground cinnamon
- 1/4 teaspoon ground nutmeg
- 1/4 teaspoon ground allspice
- 1/4 cup raisins or currants (optional)
- 1/4 cup shredded coconut (optional)
- Butter or cooking spray for greasing the baking dish

For the Rum Sauce (Optional):

- 1/2 cup butter
- 1/2 cup brown sugar
- 1/4 cup dark rum
- 1/4 cup water

Instructions:

Preheat the Oven:
- Preheat your oven to 350°F (175°C). Grease a baking dish with butter or cooking spray.

Prepare Bread Cubes:
- Cut the bread into cubes, and place them in the greased baking dish.

Prepare the Custard Mixture:
- In a mixing bowl, whisk together the milk, coconut milk, brown sugar, beaten eggs, vanilla extract, ground cinnamon, ground nutmeg, and ground allspice until well combined.

Pour Over Bread Cubes:
- Pour the custard mixture over the bread cubes in the baking dish. Allow it to sit for about 10-15 minutes, allowing the bread to absorb the liquid.

Add Optional Ingredients:

- If using, sprinkle raisins or currants and shredded coconut over the bread mixture. Gently fold them into the mixture.

Bake:
- Bake in the preheated oven for approximately 40-45 minutes or until the top is golden brown and the custard is set. A toothpick inserted into the center should come out clean.

Prepare Rum Sauce (Optional):
- In a saucepan, melt butter over medium heat. Stir in brown sugar until dissolved.
- Add dark rum and water, stirring continuously until the mixture thickens slightly. Remove from heat.

Serve:
- Once the bread pudding is baked, let it cool slightly before serving. Drizzle the optional rum sauce over individual servings if desired.

Enjoy:
- St. Lucian Bread Pudding is delicious served warm or at room temperature. Enjoy the rich flavors and local spices in this delightful Caribbean dessert.

This St. Lucian Bread Pudding captures the essence of the region's flavors, making it a comforting and sweet treat for any occasion.

Unique Treats:

Jamaican Solomon Gundy: Spicy fish spread.

Ingredients:

- 1 cup salted fish (codfish or mackerel), soaked and flaked
- 1 small onion, finely chopped
- 1/2 cup scallions (green onions), finely chopped
- 1/2 cup red bell pepper, finely chopped
- 2 cloves garlic, minced
- 1 Scotch bonnet pepper, finely chopped (adjust to taste)
- 1 teaspoon fresh thyme leaves
- 1/2 teaspoon ground allspice
- 1/4 teaspoon ground black pepper
- 1/4 cup vegetable oil
- Juice of 1 lime or lemon
- 1 tablespoon Worcestershire sauce
- Salt to taste
- Crackers or bread for serving

Instructions:

Prepare Salted Fish:
- If using salted fish, soak it in water overnight or for several hours to remove excess salt. Boil the fish until it's tender, then flake it into small pieces.

Prepare Vegetables:
- Finely chop the onion, scallions, red bell pepper, garlic, and Scotch bonnet pepper.

Sauté Aromatics:
- In a pan, heat vegetable oil over medium heat. Sauté the chopped onion, scallions, red bell pepper, garlic, and Scotch bonnet pepper until the vegetables are softened.

Add Flaked Fish:
- Add the flaked salted fish to the sautéed vegetables. Mix well to combine.

Season:

- Season the mixture with fresh thyme, ground allspice, ground black pepper, lime or lemon juice, Worcestershire sauce, and salt to taste. Stir to incorporate the flavors.

Cook:
- Continue cooking the mixture for an additional 5-7 minutes, stirring occasionally. Allow the flavors to meld.

Adjust and Cool:
- Taste and adjust the seasoning if needed. Remove the mixture from heat and let it cool to room temperature.

Serve:
- Once cooled, serve Jamaican Solomon Gundy on crackers or bread. It can be enjoyed as a spread or dip.

Note:

- Adjust the amount of Scotch bonnet pepper based on your spice tolerance. You can also remove the seeds for less heat.
- Solomon Gundy can be refrigerated in an airtight container for a few days.

Enjoy the bold and spicy flavors of Jamaican Solomon Gundy as a tasty appetizer or snack with a Caribbean flair!

Puerto Rican Mofongo: Mashed plantains with garlic and pork.

Ingredients:

For the Mofongo:

- 4 green plantains, peeled and cut into 1-inch pieces
- 4 cloves garlic, minced
- 1/2 cup pork cracklings (chicharrones) or bacon, finely chopped
- Salt, to taste
- Vegetable oil, for frying

For the Garlic Mojo Sauce:

- 3 cloves garlic, minced
- 1/2 cup extra-virgin olive oil
- 1 teaspoon vinegar (white or apple cider)
- Salt and pepper, to taste

Instructions:

For the Mofongo:

Fry Plantains:
- Heat vegetable oil in a deep pan or skillet over medium heat. Fry the plantain pieces until they are golden brown on all sides. Remove them and place them on a paper towel to drain excess oil.

Make Mofongo Base:
- In a large mortar or a sturdy bowl, place a handful of fried plantain pieces along with minced garlic and a pinch of salt. Mash the ingredients together using a pestle or the back of a spoon.

Add Pork Cracklings:
- Incorporate the chopped pork cracklings or bacon into the mashed plantains. Continue mashing until you achieve a smooth and well-mixed consistency.

Shape Mofongo Balls:

- With damp hands, shape the mashed plantains and pork into golf ball-sized rounds. You can also use a cup to shape the mofongo.

For the Garlic Mojo Sauce:
- In a small saucepan, heat extra-virgin olive oil over medium heat. Add minced garlic and sauté until it becomes fragrant but not browned.

Season and Finish Sauce:
- Add vinegar to the garlic-infused oil and season with salt and pepper. Stir well and let it cook for an additional minute. Remove from heat.

Serve:
- Arrange the mofongo balls on a plate and drizzle the garlic mojo sauce over the top.

Enjoy:
- Puerto Rican Mofongo is typically served as a side dish or accompaniment to meat or seafood dishes. Enjoy the rich flavors of mashed plantains and garlic with the added crunch of pork cracklings.

Mofongo is a beloved Puerto Rican dish that showcases the versatility of plantains and the savory goodness of garlic and pork. It's a flavorful addition to any Puerto Rican meal!

www.ingramcontent.com/pod-product-compliance
Lightning Source LLC
LaVergne TN
LVHW081552060526
838201LV00054B/1873